Charles George Herbermann

The History of Ancient Vinland

Charles George Herbermann

The History of Ancient Vinland

ISBN/EAN: 9783337328252

Printed in Europe, USA, Canada, Australia, Japan

Cover: Foto ©ninafisch / pixelio.de

More available books at **www.hansebooks.com**

INTRODUCTION.

The work of Torfaeus, a learned Icelander, which is here presented was the first book in which the story of the discovery of Vinland by the Northmen was made known to general readers. After the appearance of his work, the subject slumbered, until Rafn in this century attempted to fix the position of the Vinland of Northern accounts. Since that time scholars have been divided. Our leading historians, George Bancroft, Hildreth, Winsor, Elliott, Palfrey, regard voyages by the Norsemen southward from Greenland as highly probable, but treat the sagas as of no historical value, and the attempt to trace the route of the voyages, and fix the localities of places mentioned, as idle, with such vague indications as these early accounts, committed to writing long after the events described, can possibly afford. Toulmin Smith, Beamish, Reeves and others accepted the Norseman story as authentic, and Dr. B. F. De Costa, Horsford and Baxter are now the prominent advocates and adherents of belief in the general accuracy of the Vinland narratives.

As early as 1073 Adam of Bremen spoke of Vinland, a country where grape vines grew wild, and in 1671 Montanus, followed in 1702 by Campanius, the chronicler of New Sweden, alluded to its discovery. Peringskjold in 1697 published some of the sagas and thus brought the question more definitively before scholars; but Torfaeus, a man well versed in the history of his native island, in the book here given collected from the priestly and monastic writings all that was accessible in his day. Produced now in English, his History of Vinland will add to the literature of the subject, and with the volume of Dr. De Costa give the student almost all the material for examination. Torfaeus first proposed the statement of the length of the day as a means of fixing the position of Vinland which he believed to be near Newfoundland.

Dr. Winsor says: "Of the interpreters of this ancient lore Torfaeus has been long looked upon as a characteristic exemplar."

Some of the earlier advocates of the Vinland story found corroborative evidence in the stone mill at Newport, the inscriptions on Dighton rock, and the bronze or copper found with a fair haired skeleton. These have been wisely abandoned as utterly untrustworthy.

The narratives are vague, and it has been made an objection that the only natives described are evidently men of of Esquimaux race, not our Indians. This is really an evidence in favor of the accounts. The country of Vinland was known and referred to before the days of Columbus. If the narratives had been invented after the exploration of our coast, and with knowledge of its actual inhabitants the writers would have placed Algonquins there, not Esquimaux.

We know too little of the movement of the great American nations to be able to write the whole story, but we know some facts. The early settlers in Greenland found no Skraelings, or Esquimaux there and they did not appear till near the middle of the fourteenth century. They were evidently forced northward. Jacques Cartier found at Gaspé and in possession of the valley of the St. Lawrence tribes of the Huron Iroquois family. All the vocabulary and words given by him are of their language. He gives no Algonquin or Esquimaux terms. Yet when Champlain settled Quebec less than a century afterwards these Huron Iroquois had fallen back up the St. Lawrence to Lake Ontario and were in possession of the territory south and west of the lake. The whole valley of the St. Lawrence and the Atlantic Coast to Chesapeake Bay were held by Algonquin tribes. These at the north warred with a tribe to whom they gave the name of Esquimaux or Raw Meat Eaters. The Esquimaux held their own in Labrador in 1612(Biard, "Relation de la Nouvelle France,") and in 1659 were still at war with the

INTRODUCTION.

Micmacs of Gaspé, (Relation, 1659). That they occupied the coast lower down before they were forced northward into Greenland, would seem therefore most probable. Yet if these accounts of voyages to Vinland were invented or built up on a few vague indications, the inventors could not have been such philosophic ethnologists as to place Esquimaux in New England. The accessible material at their hands would have led them to place Algonquins on the coast.

Rude implements found in the interglacial Jersey drift have been held by C. C. Abbot to have been associated with a people of the Esquimaux stock, so that Esquimaux may have occupied the coast below Sandy Hook.

Christian Irish had preceded the Northmen to the Faroe Islands, as Dicuil, an Irish monk, makes clear, and to Iceland; but the Scandinavians who settled Iceland and Greenland, who made voyages thence southward were just emerging from heathenism into the light of Christianity. Catholic bishops and priests, the mass and prayers are mentioned in the narratives, and one of the heroines makes a pilgrimage to Rome.

This fixes to a certain extent the time of the alleged voyages, for the time of the introduction of Christianity into Iceland and Greenland is fairly well authenticated.

JOHN GILMARY SHEA.

TRANSLATOR'S PREFACE.

Thormod Torfason, or as he latinized his name, Thormodus Torfaeus, the author of our History of Vinland, was born on the island of Engoe on the north coast of Iceland, in 1640. At this time Iceland formed a part of the kingdom of Denmark. Accordingly Torfason went to Copenhagen for his education. There the young man's brilliant abilities soon found recognition. He was hardly twenty years of age when the Danish King, Frederick III, who took a deep interest in the early history of the Northmen, appointed him *interpres regius* for northern antiquities. Two years later (1662) he was sent to Iceland, partly to perfect his knowledge of the ancient language of his native land, partly to gather Icelandish manuscripts for the royal library at Copenhagen. With the aid of Bishop Brynjolf Sveinsson, whom Torfaeus himself calls the most learned of all the bishops of Skalholt up to his time, he carried out his commission successfully; as a reward he was appointed secretary of the bailiwick of Stavanger in the south of Norway (1664). But Torfaeus was not destined to bury his talents in the administration of a small Norwegian country place. He remained there only three years; then he was recalled to Copenhagen and appointed Curator of the Royal Cabinet of Antiquities. While holding this position he again visited Iceland and subsequently made a voyage to Holland. During this voyage he proved that he had not only the love of learning of his Icelandish forefathers, but also the violent spirit of the old Vikings. Attacked by a man Torfaeus struck him down and killed him. He was tried and condemned to death. His distinction as a scholar however, led the King to pardon him, though he was obliged to pay a heavy fine and lost his place as the head of the royal Cabinet (1673. He went to

Norway and became more absorbed than ever before in the study of the Eddas, of the Sagas and of Northern Antiquities in general. On the death of Frederick III, his successor, Christian V, named Torfaeus Royal Historiographer of Norway and made him a member of the commission on education. The fruits of his studies now appeared in rapid succession. His History of the Faroe Islands appeared in 1695, and was followed (1697) by the History of the Orkneys, and the Table of the Chiefs and Kings of Denmark (1702). In 1705 was published the History of Vinland, which now for the first time appears in an English dress. The History of Ancient Greenland (1706) and the *Trifolium Historicum* (1707) led up to the publication of his principal work, the History of Norway in four large volumes (1711). This was the last of his works that appeared during his lifetime. But so great was the esteem in which he was held by Northern scholars, that many years after his death, in 1777, his unpublished miscellaneous papers were printed by his admiring countrymen. Torfaeus died in 1719.

All Torfaeus' works were written in Latin. Hence, while John Peringskjold was perhaps the first to revive the memory of the Norse discovery of America in his Swedish translation of the Heimskringla, (1697) yet Torfason's History of Vinland first made known the claims of the Northmen to European scholars. The body of his history, as he himself tells us in his preface, is based on two old Icelandish manuscripts, the celebrated Flatey Book, known as No. 1005 fol. of the Old Royal Collection in Copenhagen, and on a paper manuscript, No. 678 in the same collection. On the former are based Chapters I to VIII, of the History of Vinland, on the latter Chapters IX to XIV. The Flatey Book, so called because it was long preserved on the island of Flatey, near Iceland, is a remarkable work. It is in the main a history of the Kings of Norway, written on vellum, and fills 1700 closely packed pages of print at thirty-nine lines per page. Two priests, John Thordsson and Magnus Thorhallson, undertook this encyclopaedic work for an Icelander named John Haconson. Like most mediæval records, therefore, the story of the finding of Vinland by the Northmen has been preserved for us by Catholic priests. The Flatey Book was probably written at Widedals-tunga, near the monastery of Thingeyrar, whence the authors probably drew many of the manuscripts from which the material for their work was drawn. The learned Norse scholar Gudbrand Vigfussen, in the preface to his edition of the Orkneyinga Saga (Vol. I, p. XXV) has proved by an ingenious course of reasoning, that the manuscript was finished in 1387, about three hundred and seventy-five years after the discovery of Vinland. The version of this discovery, found in the Flatey Book, usually called the Saga of Eric the Red, was, however, taken from older manuscripts, so that we cannot say, when it was first written down from tradition.

The second account of the discovery of Vinland, taken by Torfaeus from N. 768, O. R. C. of Copenhagen, is usually entitled the Saga of Thorfinn Karlsefne. Torfason's manuscript is much younger than the Flatey Book. But since his death another parchment manuscript was found in the Arne-Magnaean Collection of Copenhagen, being No. 544 of that collection, which seems to be the original of Torfaeus' paper manuscript. This old parchment proved to be even older than the Flatey Book, being ascribed by palaeographers to the end of the thirteenth or the beginning of the fourteenth century. Accordingly, if age is to decide, this version should be even more authoritative than the Flatey Book.

Torfaeus' narrative is based upon the manuscripts he had before him. Indeed, it may be said without exaggeration, that whole pages of his History are fairly literal translations of the Flatey Book, or of the Karlsefne Saga. He makes no attempt to reconcile nor to explain the discrepancies of the two versions of his story, though the differences are neither slight nor unimportant. To him the account of the discovery of Vinland, and found in the Saga of Eric the Red, seemed preferable to that of the Karlsefne Saga, because it is simpler and more probable. Perhaps his judgment may have been influenced by his own connection with the Flatey book, for it was by his hands that Bishop Brynolf

Steinsson sent the royal volume to King Frederick III (1662). Still his opinion has been endorsed by many scholars since his time and especially by Carl Christian Rafu, the editor of the *Antiquitates Americanae*, who first printed the Icelandic originals of the two Sagas. Of late, however, there seems to be a turn in the tide and Mr. Reeves, the author of 'The Finding of Wineland the Good," (Oxford, 1890) is outspoken In his advocacy of the Karlsefne Saga, as contained in the very old parchment Codex, A. M. No. 544. He supports his views by showing that other Icelandic manuscripts, containing brief accounts of the discovery of Vinland, or allusions thereto, agree with this version rather than with the story of the Flatey Book. However that may be, the reader after carefully perusing the two versions will see the importance of reconciling or at least explaining their discrepancies; and this may not prove impossible. At all events, so much is certain: Thormod Torfason has given a fairly full and correct, and an honest history of the discovery of Vinland, as given in the old Norse records. He has concealed no difficulties, nor omitted to present his readers with all the evidence available in his day. Nor has much been added to this evidence since, except a few extracts from Are Thorgillson's Islendingabok and from the Landnamabok, which confirm Torfaeus' documents, without adding anything essentially new. Our History of Vinland, therefore, has not outgrown its usefulness, though it is the earliest work, that made known to modern scholars the tale of the discovery of America by the Northmen.

HISTORY OF
ANCIENT VINLAND,
OR OF
PART OF NORTH AMERICA.

In which is reviewed the Reason of the Name; the Position of the Land is determined from the length of the Days in winter; the Fertility of the Soil, and the barbarous character of the Inhabitants, the temporary sojourn of its Discoverers and their Exploits, the Name of the adjacent Lands and their Appearance, are set forth from ancient Icelandic Sources brought to Light

BY

THORMOD TORFAEUS,

ROYAL HISTORIOGRAPHER OF NORWAY.

COPENHAGEN :
Printed at the press of his Royal Majesty and of the University
1705
At the Author's Expense.

APPROBATION.

The character of our age is to extol what is new, neglecting the old. Therefore not so much the indulgence as the applause of the public is due to those who, like the most noble author of this work, rescue from darkness and bring to light ancient history and geography. Copenhagen, Sept. 2nd, in the year 1705.

P. VINDINGIUS.

To the most Illustrious and most Excellent
Hero
LORD FREDERICK DE GABEL, LORD OF BREGENTUED,
Golden Knight
of the Order of the Danebrog,
Secret Counselor of State and Justice
of His Sacred Majesty of Denmark and Norway,
Lord Lieutenant of Norway,
Royal Governor
of the District of Aggershus and Ferroe.

MOST ILLUSTRIOUS AND EXCELLENT LORD.

The year, immediately preceding the present, the fourth of this century, has been everywhere consecrated in eternal records as most memorable, the year when the most august sovereign of these realms and their hereditary King, our most clement Lord, Frederick the Fourth, accompanied, among other most illustrious, most noble and great ministers by your Excellency also, most illustrious Lord Lieutenant, most mercifully deigned after the example of his great father, of most glorious memory, Christian the Fifth, to visit his realm, from its easternmost boundaries even to Nidarosia, and was universally received with the most marked enthusiasm of the whole people and of all classes, with festive acclaim and the most earnest wishes, the most ardent prayers and supplications for the perpetual safety and lasting prosperity of his Majesty. Surely parts of the fifth and sixth days of July, and the intervening night which was turned into bright sunlight, more than other times, shone upon me most auspiciously, when on that royal visit our Sovereign permitted this obscure and humble village to be selected for his stopping-place, where it was our privilege to behold with due reverence the most kind and gentle features of his father and grand-father, so to say, revived in his most serene countenance, and after a long interval to recall them more clearly than in any mirror that glitters with bright colors. But when at the same time your Excellency brought up the questions of the exploration of ancient Greenland, and of the establishment of trade in Davis' Straits, I answered to the first part only and disapproved of a route so often passed over as little fit for reaching the end aimed at; being bidden to point out one more suitable, I put off the expression of my opinion, being hindered by the presence of his Royal Majesty. On the following morning I set it forth to your most illustrious Excellency most briefly, owing to your haste. So far was your Excellency from finding fault therewith, that you even deigned to publish, and afterwards to praise it, when not so long ago I explained it more fully in a letter to your Excellency; finally I inserted it in my Preface to Ancient Greenland. The second question, on exploring Davis' Straits, is sufficiently answered both by home precedents known to many and by foreign precedents; for it is proved that it has been visited long ago by vessels from Holland, and according to the testimony of Arngrim, from England also.

Finally, I humbly offer to your Excellency the present treatise on VINLAND, in order to testify and express most positively my feelings of most submissive devotion and outspoken respect. For as the superintendence and supreme government of all Norway, which you administer with the greatest care and success, has been intrusted to your Excellency, you are wont to enquire most carefully, among other things which relate to its welfare, what fame this people has attained in past ages. Although the most flourishing realms of our part of the globe bear complete witness to our fame, yet this is crowned by the glory of first opening through its colonists parts of the New World, among which this (Vinland) is by no means the least. I admit indeed, that the record thereof which has come down to us is very scant; for though mention is made therein of a great number of wild beasts and of traffic in their skins, yet there is no specific account, so that they note neither the varieties of birds nor of fishes, mention very few species of trees and none at all of plants, nor any other things relating to the description of the countries. But in as much as it does not lie in the power of any historian to furnish himself with richer materials than have been handed down to him, your Excellency will pardon my deficiency in this respect; for I know the moderation of your Excellency's mind to be such, that even if I had made a rather thoughtless mistake, you would yet extend to me your kind indulgence for my rashness. But as the mistake is not mine, trusting in your Excellency's kindness, of which I have heretofore received various marks, I most humbly submit to the patronage of your Excellency my work, such as it is, as well as myself, and request for both your favor, kindness, good will and protection. That the Lord of Heaven may plentifully grant your Excellency all prosperity in the fullest measure worthy of Heaven, I sincerely pray with suppliant mind, hand and pen.

Your most illustrious Excellency's

Most humble servant,

T. TORFAEUS.

PREFACE TO THE READER.

From the creation and renovation of the world, if you accept the Sacred Record, up to the present time, I know not what more important event has been handed down in history than the discovery of the New World; though some ascribe the glory thereof to the ancient Phoenicians and their descendants, the Carthaginians, yet they lack the undoubted testimony necessary to convince all fully of its correctness; but even if this were completely admitted, yet they achieved no less glory, who restored it to perpetual light after being buried in oblivion for so many centuries thereafter. The fame of that immense achievement for a long time appeared to have been won by a man who has never been sufficiently praised, Christopher Columbus, a Genoese, who in the year of grace, 1492, discovered a part thereof. Nor did Americus Vespucius, of Florence, who set foot on it four years after, under the auspices of Emanuel, King of Portugal, carry off less renown; nay, he gained even greater glory. Some, however, claim for themselves the honor of discovering those countries in former ages; the Venetian brothers, for instance, Nicholas and Antonio surnamed Zeni, in the year 1380 after Christ, the last year of the Norwegian King Haco, the Sixth of that name, as he insisted, in truth the Seventh; and two centuries before these Madoc, son of Gwineth, (brother of the Prince of Wales) who is said to have led colonies to Canada and Florida, about the year 1170. But from the present work it will be clear that none of these (even should what is related of the Zeni be true, whereof hereafter) could claim for themselves the glory of first discovering America, nor could posterity justly and fairly claim it for them. The Greenlanders, colonists of Iceland and to some extent the Icelanders themselves, first of all snatched this glory from both, and indeed from Madoc, 150 years and more before his time. They did this in such a way that they have not only secured for themselves the undying honor and glory of discovering and of hastily settling Vinland, but also that of finally making it known far and wide and of publishing the Christian religion throughout the neighboring Albania or Great Ireland, (for this could not have been done before by others.) Therefore, kind reader, behold these two accounts of the discovery of Vinland, which for the present I offer you, not such as I should wish them to be, but such as they have been handed down to me, and as I can repeat them. Both are scant and slight; neither is entirely consistent with the other. I repeat them rather to strengthen my present thesis, and to leave the position of the country (Vinland) to be investigated by others from the facts here set down, and to reclaim for the descendants of the first occupants any right that may have accrued to them from that occupation than from a hope to satisfy you, even by both stories together. The first narrative, extending from the beginning to Chapter VIII is found in the Codex Flateyensis, in the history of King Olaf Triggvin, and, as it seems, in some other old manuscripts also. Having borrowed it from some one of these, the most distinguished head of the Royal Swedish Archives, John Peringskjold, inserted it in the history of the Norse Kings, the Heimskringla, from chapter 104 to chapter 112, whilst they do not exist in the manuscripts commonly ascribed to Snorro Sturleson, to wit: the Kringla or Jofraskinna, which I have borrowed from the Library of the Church of the Most Holy Trinity, at Copenhagen.

The second narrative, a most famous antiquary of the last century, the Icelander Bjorn of Skardsa, collected from ancient documents, and chiefly from that most perfect book on the Origins of Iceland, by the jurist Hauk, who died in the year 1334, and from various traditions of later times. Both agree in saying that at the end of the tenth century after the birth of the Saviour, or at the beginning of the following century, Vinland was seen and soon after discovered; and hence all doubt on this question is dispelled. Their differences in other particulars are so far from destroying the fundameutal parts of the story, that they rather strengthen them : for in as much as they agree in essentials, their differences in regard to details, and those more minute details, readily show that the different writers did not conspire to hand down falsehood, and moreover that they did not copy each others' writings. On this argument that most distinguished man, Olaf Rudbecke in the second paragraph of the first chapter of his Atlant. discourses learnedly: from him I shall cite a few words. For after promising a short dissertation on the abstruse method of writing, involved in fables and riddles, he adds: "But indeed, others, too, may be found who will regard not only this abstruse method of writing, but history setting forth everything in the plainest language, as fiction, especially if it happen that different writers disagree in some particulars. But if such writers are compelled at different times to relate one and the same event, do we believe that they will always use the same order, the same number of words, and precisely the same enumeration of the minutest particulars? By no means! Truly not even the four Evangelists agree thus among themselves, however wonderful may be their agreement in truth and on all the chief points of the heavenly teaching. The books of Kings also and the so called Paralipomena in the Old Testament, although they relate the events of the same period, yet so differ in language and at times in the fulness of the facts, that to obtain a complete and perfect version of the history, they must sometimes mutually complement and help each other. Therefore to attain the truth, it will certainly suffice to trace out the essential features of the story ; the disagreement of writers in lesser particulars, is too unimportant to obscure the truth, when it shines by its own light, a principle which will be illustrated more fully by a famous example. Moses has given us by far the most accurate account of the deluge and has set forth most carefully its occasion, causes, details, chronology and the story of the men that survived it ; the same event was afterward, by the faith of tradition, made known to the pagans also ; but both on account of the length of time and the somewhat doubtful good faith of the writers, the story has many and considerable breaks, some interpolations, as well as many changes." Then after setting forth the various versions of the catastrophe he finally adds: "What of the fact that any one who is willing to consider these things carefully, will see clearly this inference, which while it was not before thought of by any one, yet exceeds all mere probability: that there underlies the narrative of these writers, though they differ from one another, a certain most undoubted substratum of agreement and truth, placed there so to say by divine Providence; for as we regard those who relate the same fact in precisely the same words and according to the same arrangement and style, as pilferers of other's work (except one who precedes the rest in time) so also, had the Chaldeans, Scythians, Greeks and Egyptians agreed entirely with Moses or any other historian of the deluge, both in language and details, they could never have escaped the same criticism, and in that case the whole story would seem to depend on the testimony not of many but of a single witness. But whenever different writers differently set forth the same event, in regard to which they agree with one another, it is evident at once that the same fact was beheld or perceived by several persons, but was not handed down to posterity by all with equal truth in all respects nor with the like care. Meanwhile however, the pith of the story will be confirmed by several and will not admit of doubt on our part."

But I am excusing the variations of the present narratives in a larger preface than is necessary, for they are very slight and can be examined with very little trouble.

I. The CODEX FLATEYENSIS relates that the new countries were seen, but not entered, by Bjarne, the Icelander, that they were explored and endowed with names by Leif. Bjorn of Skardsa is silent concerning Bjarne, but the rest he admits; there is a slight difference of opinion whether Leif came to the new lands when returning from Norway, or whether he sailed from Greenland especially, in order to explore them.

II. The Codex Flateyensis says that Thorvald, the son of Eric the Red, next visited them and was finally pierced with an arrow by the Skraelings. Bjorn tells a far less probable story, for he introduces the fabulous country of the unipedes.

III. The Codex Flateyensis says that after Thorvald's death, his brother Thorstein undertook a voyage thither: Bjorn places that voyage before Thorvald's death. The Codex is more trustworthy, for it first tells of his wife's death, of the marriage contract, and lastly how she married Karlsefne.

IV. The Codex Flateyensis describes a third expedition to Vinland under the leadership of Karlsefne: the third, for Thorstein had not reached Vinland. Bjorn recounts the story more simply, yet he errs in counting Thorvald among his companions, for he had been previously slain; nor is it more worthy of belief, that he gave their names to Markland and Helluland; to other places he certainly appears to have given names.

V. The Codex Flateyensis alone relates the fourth voyage to Vinland, which Bjorn did not find mentioned in Hauk's book; and yet it is quite probable, for it was the last; and Freidis, the daughter of Eric the Red, seems to have been present with both, and during the last to have become mad and to have acted in a ferocious way. The minute details I shall not examine, for it is not of such importance whether the discovery of those countries or the death of Eric the Red is placed one or two years sooner or later, and the like. What may be a matter of controversy regarding the position of Vinland I have discussed in a note with all possible diligence. For it must be sought in that part of the North American continent where the productions here described grow or which the descriptions fit, and where the character of the country is found agreeing therewith; but whether these suit the character of the climate in which Estotiland lies according to the common opinion, I greatly doubt.

I am not unaware that Buno in his notes to Philip Cluverius' Introduction to Universal Geography, book VI, chap. 12, denies that Estotiland is to be found in those parts of America (he describes Canada), as well as that the island of Frisland ever existed in the adjacent part of the ocean.

PREFACE.

Henry Kipping, Pol. Institutes, book I, chap. 20, p. 173., not only supports him, but denies that they are located anywhere, in the following words: "Frisland and Estotiland exist nowhere, whatever the Venetian Zeni in their Sea Voyage may have wished to make us believe;" but Buno in the notes of the afore-mentioned work, book III, chap. 20, paragraph 4, page 209, contradicts himself and says that Greenland is separated by Davis' Strait from the American Estotiland. For my part I have no quarrel in regard to the name, since Sanson d' Abbeville and more recent geographers regard the new land of Labrador, adjoining Hudson Bay as identical with Estotiland; that it is not the same, however as the Estotiland, which the Zeni describe, I suspect from the fact that they state that it (Estotiland) lies more than a thousand miles to the west of Frisland. Since Frisland however is usually placed in 62° latitude and about 342° of longitude, whilst Estotiland is placed 58° of latitude and about 290° of longitude, they (the Zeni) must have proceeded farther towards America and have found there the Estotiland which they describe. This land without doubt was large, since it was little smaller than Iceland, but superior in fertility, inasmuch as it was situated in a milder climate, very rich, and abounding in all kinds of products, even gold and various metals; remarkable for its cities, castles, towns and splendid structures. But I do not know whether this fits those barbarous tribes in those times. There is besides the published description of the island of Drogio and of the vast country extending thence towards the south and southwest, which present the features of another continent; these statements suggest the opinion that they were carried to parts of North America, and that those who afterwards discovered the furthest parts of North America, convinced that they had reached the same Estotiland, of which they (the Zeni) speak, adopted the name, though the position was different; certainly the construction of boats, quite well known to those tribes (the Skraelings) and described exactly in this document, an art perhaps wholly unknown to such distant nations at that time, would also convince me that those brothers were carried to that part of the ocean and reached some part of America; if I were sure that their book was printed before the knowledge of those tribes (the Americans) was wide spread and furnished impostors full material for fiction and the power of inventing fables. Above all, on account of the gross and unskilful concoction and wonderful stories with which it is filled, I think that the book was compiled in more recent times under the name of such distinguished men, for the purpose of gaining authority. I think this is so because I know the bare-faced impudence of Bleyker and the shameless boldness of Martinerius, not to mention other names; both of these, with astounding temerity, printed and published their travels, itineraries to Iceland and Greenland, (and the latter pretends that in the time of Frederick the III, of most glorious memory, he traveled thither, though I am not certain that the one ever saw Iceland and either of them Greenland), they were believed by many and the latter to no slight degree gained credence with that most distinguished man, Olaf Rudbecke, and won his respect. It is miraculous that the chief city of Frisland should have abounded in such quantities of fish, that Flemings as well as Britons, besides English, Scots, Norwegians and Danes imported them in great numbers, and the islanders accumulated immense wealth therefrom; that in the annals of these nations there is no mention of them, and not even a trace of Frisland and of the trade with its inhabitants; that not even the Norwegians and Icelanders, who, frequently stopping in their country and at their courts, fought in their wars while others were engaged in commerce, have any knowledge that Frisland was ever under their power, and that it was wrested from them by Zichinnus, and that—a thing unusual with kings—it was never, I shall not say, recovered, but not even sought after or attacked with a view to restore it to its allegiance. You retort that it is mentioned by geographers, for Johannes Laurentius Ananias in his FABRICA DEL MONDO, informs us that in his day it greatly abounded in fish and for that reason was frequented by Scotch and British merchants, and that he was informed by Jonas, the Breton, a relative of Jacques Cartier, who first discovered New France in the year 1554, that he (Jonas) had himself entered it and that its inhabitants are very polite and kind towards foreigners; and this is confirmed by John Boterus. Moreover, John Antony Maginus bears witness that in his day the English traded there to the great advantage of the islanders, and that they called the island West England. Ortelius also mentions it on page 90, Berti on page 56, as well as John Miritius in a geographical treatise published in the year 1590; whose words Arngrim Jonas quoted on page 190 of book III, of his CRYMOGAEA adding his own opinion on the several points. But Mercator and Hondius going further, set down the cities of Frisland with their proper names: 1° the capital of the same name as the island. 2 Sorand; 3 Ocibar; 4 Sanestol; 5 Crodme; 6 Doffais; 7 Campo; 8 Rane; 9 Bondendon; 10 Rovea; 11 Andefort; 12 Cabaru. Small islands near Frisland are also enumerated: 1° Ilofo; 2 Jedeve; 3 Venai; 4 Monaco; 5 Spirige; 6 Streme; 7 Ibini; 8 Duime; 9 Porlanda. That these statements were read by those most learned men Buno and Kipping, I have not the slightest doubt: still they could not be induced to attach any importance to them; nor were more recent geographers moved to give them a place in their descriptions. For my part, I who have gathered the history of Norway from all kinds of documents worthy of credit, have certainly nowhere found any mention of this Frisland, and therefore deny that it was ever subject to the Norwegians; whatever is there (in Zeno) recounted of Zichinnus' war with the Norwegians, must therefore be placed among the myths Nor is what he wrote of Iceland and the neighboring islands, more probable; for it is contrary to the experience of all ages. On these points the reader may consult Arngrim Jonas, in his description of Iceland, part 2, memb. 2, page m. 140 and ff., as well as Theodore Thorlake's Dissertation on Iceland: these will fully satisfy him.

Therefore, passing over the absurdities, which that writer has published about Greenland, so different from the description of Ivar Berius, a man most familar with those matters, and ignoring the other tales which he added, for example, concerning Grisland, Estland and Icaria and the unknown and never discovered situation of those lands, we conclude that the glory of first discovering Vinland belongs, whole and undiminished, to the Greenlanders and Icelanders, the descendants of the Norsemen, and we award to them not only the glory of discovering it but also of making known the Christian religion to those peoples. For Are Marson is said to have been driven by storms to Great Ireland near Vinland, which (Great Ireland) they otherwise call ALBANIA or HVITRA MANNA LAND, and is distant from Ireland a voyage of six days towards the west according to the Book of Origins of Iceland, part 2, chap. 22, page 64. This distance does not differ greatly from the computations of Philip Cluverius, who reckons the distance thence to Canada at 200 miles (Book VI, chap. 2, p. 419). He (Are Marson) is there said to have been converted to Christianity. This happened before the year 1000 after Christ, and before Christianity was introduced into Iceland, for he was the great grandson of Ulf Skialg, who first settled Reikyanes and as at that time neither Greenland nor much less the above mentioned Great Ireland was Christianized, the sacred mysteries of Christianity which he then embraced must have been taught him whilst he was detained there (in Great Ireland) but he was detained there as long as he lived. This, I conjecture, was done by Jones, Jonas, or John, an Irish Bishop, who whilst Isleif, the first Bishop of all Iceland, was presiding over the Cathedral of Schalholt, came thither between the years 1056 and 1080 and is said to have gone thence to Vinland, to have preached the Gospel, and having gained over many to Christ, to have finally been tortured and killed; on this subject, see chap. XVI, of our Vinland. At that time therefore, not only Vinland, which was then found worthy to be spoken of by Adam of Bremen in his writings, but also this very Great Ireland became known, so that this story of the aforesaid Are, which we have just recounted was taken by Icelanders from the Relation of Thorfinn, Earl of the Orkneys, who died in the year 1064, published in Iceland and adopted into literature. Hence, we readily infer that even more Christians from Ireland and elsewhere went thither from the time those lands first became known, to propagate their religion, though the Icelanders and Greenlanders were not aware of this. This, however, has been recorded by them, that subsequently in the next century, that is to say in the year 1121, Eric, the first Bishop of Greenland, visited Vinland, as a place well known at that time, (for what other purpose, I ask, except to labor there for Christ?) and that the opinion prevailed that he perished during that visit. But in the chapter quoted above, it is mentioned, that long before him, Bjarn the champion of Breidavik reached, if not Vinland, certainly some other part of North America, and that by his aid and influence, his countryman Gunnlaug Gudleifson with his whole ship's company was saved from imminent danger of life. These are the men, who, as Sanson d'Abbeville in his description of Virginia, page 14, suggests, were taken by a certain Gascon for Gascons; for he writes that he (the Gascon) assured him (Sanson) that he would prove that Gascons had been in New France four or five hundred years before Baron de Lery or John Verazzani came there; now, the former came there in 1518, the latter in 1542. As this time agrees precisely with the period when those countries were first discovered, the story adds great authority to our story. I shall say nothing of the part of New France bordering on the sea, called Norumberga, as Cluverius thinks, from the city of the same name, which name Buno in his notes to the same passage interprets to mean Norway or a colony led thither from Norway. It is clear that after the time of Christopher Columbus, no part of New France was settled by the Norse; perhaps the name given to the land in ancient times was preserved, but whether the city was built before the arrival of the French, I have not yet ascertained; certainly if it was founded before their time, it seems to imply the origin of the name from the tribe, if afterwards, from the country in which it lay, and that again derives its name from the old colonists. Thus it has been fully proved that that part of America became well known throughout the North and West in the eleventh century of the

Christian era. I do not know any more than others, how, during the succeeding centuries up to the time of Columbus it was plunged into the densest darkness and became again unknown. That Harold (the Bold or Imperious), the most skillful chief of the Northmen, who, as Adam of Bremen says, was about to explore it, was carried by storms to the icebound ocean of Greenland, and returned without achieving his plans, I gather from his story: had he examined its character and products more carefully, he would no doubt, after settling his quarrel with the Danes, have there found richer booty, and that too entailing neither loss nor danger; and he would have acquired wealth and power formidable to the whole North. But engaged in lengthy wars, he had no time for so great and unknown an undertaking. To explore it and Vinland as a part of it, a certain Rolf was sent in the 88th year of the thirteenth century, by Eric, the second of that name, King of Norway, surnamed PRESTAHATARA, the Priesthater, (the Greeks would translate it μισόκληρον and supplies for that voyage were exacted in the following year from the Icelanders, according to the conjecture of Arngrim (Crymogaea, Book III, p. 119 and ff.); this took place only two centuries before Columbus discovered a part of South America. What we have related above of Madoc about the year 1170, is therefore nowise absurd; for that several nations at this period sent colonies thither is probable; and I know not how Thorfinn, Earl of Orkney, otherwise acquired his knowledge of those countries, even as regards minute details, (as appears in the story of Are). On the other hand, if in those centuries (for we speak of the thirteenth century under Eric II, king of Norway) the knowledge of those lands still existed, how did it wholly escape the knowledge of Henry VII, King of England and of all his ministers two centuries later? For it is proved that Columbus first made known his plans and offered his services to this king, which he would surely not have refused, if he had known of the lands and of their vicissitudes. I am convinced that all the settlers were killed or conquered by the barbarians there; that the rest were debarred from the use of ships and unable to leave, and that if there were any additional visitors, they were treated in the same way, and that for this reason the memory of those countries and peoples, consecrated among the Icelanders only, suddenly vanished. That the Greenlanders and Icelanders fearing the violence and number of the natives, gave up the occupation of the land, not of their own accord, but against their will, we read here, and Ivar Berius bears witness that all the Western District (Vestri Bygd) of Greenland was laid waste by the Skraelings. I shall not thence conclude with the distinguished Grotius, that these tribes (the Skraelings) were the descendants of the Greenlanders, but I rather consider them the offspring of the Samoyeds, whose customs and mode of life are proved by a comparison of both to resemble those of the Skraelings; their physique and character also is very similar: both are slim of build, nor do they differ in form and features, both cover their tents and bodies with the skins of wild beasts, both alike adore the sun, both value highly the cheapest goods, mirrors, fish-hooks, knives and rattles; both are equally skilled in the use of the spear, and in unfailingly striking the mark; both eat raw flesh, whence both have a fetid stench; I shall not speak of other points of resemblance. Nor is the passage (from Asia to America), however much obstructed by the intervening mountains and deserts. entirely barred, especially to men pursuing wild animals; this passage, moreover, is afforded by bays and straits which are spanned with ice by the constant cold, as if by a bridge. Nor is there a boundless distance between the two peoples, for in the far North the degrees of latitude are smaller and the distance too, broken by the intervention of tribes near Sualbardus, as is shown in the 5th chapter of my Greenland towards the end. This origin is, furthermore proved by the animals common to both, which differ from the horses and oxen, for example, that have been brought to Greenland. These were unknown in America before the arrival of the Spaniards, and the natives were frightened by their lowing and neighing. Therefore, in conclusion, those barbarians seem to be the offspring of the Samoyeds, carried to the furthest ends of America either by some land route hitherto unknown, or in the little boats invented by themselves, (which were not endangered by the sea). And yet I should not forthwith think that the other parts of America were peopled by them, and that nations differing from them in appearance and customs were descended from them; the difference (in physique and customs) of these tribes implies a difference of origin also, and of them, I must not discourse, as they lie outside of the scope of my work. But if anyone thinks the same of the last chapter of this book which deals with the prodigies of Froda, let him know that we were led by the incidents there related to refresh the wearied spirits of our readers with a certain variety, and everybody can fix their value according to his disposition without any objection on our part. As nothing further that is worthy of mention suggests itself, do you, kind reader, read and judge kindly of these pages, whatever their value. Farewell.

HISTORY OF

ANCIENT VINLAND.

CONTENTS.

CONTENTS OF THE CHAPTERS OF THE PRESENT HISTORY OF VINLAND.

Approbation. . . page 2

Dedication. 3

Preface to the Reader. . 6

CHAPTER I.
Of the occasion of first noticing and then Discovering Vinland. 25

CHAPTER II.
Of the Discovery of Vinland by Leif. 27

CHAPTER III.
Of the Discovery of Vines and Wild Grapes and of Leif's Return. 28

CHAPTER IV.
Of the Voyage of Thorvald to Vinland, and his Expeditions to parts of it; of the findings of some persons of an unknown race; of the Murder of Thorvald and the return of his companions to their native country. 30

CHAPTER V.
Of the toilsome and fruitless voyage of Leif's brother, Thorstein, who intended to visit Vinland, of his forced return to Greenland, when the plague had broken

out, of his death and the prodigy connected with it.   32

Chapter VI.

Of the Voyage of Karlsefne to Vinland, of his traffic with the Skraelings and of the disputes thence arising, which resulted in open war.   .   .   .   34

Chapter VII.

Of the fourth Expedition to Vinland, under the leadership of Thorvald, the husband of Freydis and two Icelanders, Helge and Fimbog, of the inhuman cruelty of Freydis, of Karlsefne's return to Iceland and of his family.   .   .'   .   .   37

Chapter VIII.

Of Leif's journey to Norway to King Olaf Tryggvin, of his discovery of Vinland on his return, and of the successful preaching of the Christian religion in his native country.   41

Chapter IX.

Of the fruitless attempt of Leif's brother, Thornstein, to explore Vinland, of his return to Greenland, of his marriage with Thorbiorn's daughter, Gudrid, of her education and ancestors in Iceland.   .   .   42

Chapter X.

Of a certain prophetic woman, of her appearance and of skill in the magic (scidic) art.   .   .   .   44

Chapter XI.

Of the infectious disease that arose among Thorstein's crew, of his death and of a prodigy, of the ancient

CONTENTS. 23

mode of burial in Greenland, of the arrival of Karlsefne, and his marriage with Gudrid. . . . 47

Chapter XII.

Of Karlsefne's Voyage to Vinland, of his companions on that Expedition, viz: Bjarne, Thorhall, and Thorvard, the son-in-law of Eric the Red, and his son Thorvald. 51

Chapter XIII.

Of Thorhall, the Hunter, who is driven by storms to Iceland, and there held in bondage to the end of his life, of the further Exploration of Vinland by Karlsefne and his companions, of the land and water products there, of the dress of the Skraelings, of their traffic and of the disputes and wars thence arising, which however end in the Skraelings sustaining greater loss. 53

Chapter XIV

Of the slaying of Thorvald, the son of Eric the Red, by a one-footed man, of Karlsefne's sojourn at Straumsfiord for three winters, of the birth of his son Snorre, of the captivity of two Skraelings, of the dangerous voyage Bjarne Grimolfson in the Irish Ocean, of his honorable conduct towards a certain Icelander in extreme peril of life, of Karlsefne's return to Iceland, and his descendants. 57

Chapter XV.

Adam of Bremen's Story of Vinland, consistent with the above, and his great mistake regarding its position, whilst Olaf Rudbeck no less erroneously identifies

Vinland with Finland, and the story of the position of Great Ireland and of Are, the Icelander, and of the pitch of the Greenlanders. . . . 60

Chapter XVI.

Of the voyages to Vinland, of the Saxon Bishop Jones and of Eric, Bishop of Greenland, and concerning Gudleif Gudlangson. 62

Chapter XVII.

Of the prodigies of Froda. . . . 65

Addenda. 74

CHAPTER I.

OF THE OCCASION OF THE FIRST NOTICING AND AFTERWARDS DISCOVERING VINLAND.

The well-known Herjulf, who accompanied Eric the Red in the year 985 from Iceland, and settled Herjulfsnes, by his wife Thorgerde had a son, named Bjarne, who going in tender youth to foreign parts, acquired wealth and experience; his winters he spent alternately either abroad or with his father, and he had resolved to pass the present winter at his father's home. But when on his return to his native land he learned that his father had gone to Greenland the same summer and there settled, being a stubborn observer of customs he had once adopted, he declared, he would spend the winter in his father's house even in Greenland, though unknown to him and recently discovered; therefore he entrusted his ship to an unknown sea, unploughed by any of his sailors before him. Three days were passed in sailing, during which he saw nothing except the sky and the water, and then a northwind blowing, darkness for several days prevented his seeing anything, and made it impossible to direct the ship's course; the darkness being dispelled, they sailed a whole day and night with sails set, until an unknown land came in view. When on approaching it, they found it bare of mountains, covered with forests and low hills, they turned their ships and left it. For two days after they sped along before a south south-east wind, until another country came in sight, level, and full of woods; when the captain recognized that it differed from the mountainous and snow-clad landscape of Greenland, though the sailors begged him to land and take in water and wood, and though the wind was still, he yet did not permit himself to be prevailed upon, for which he even incurred some blame. When he had departed thence, taking advantage of a south-west wind, which for three days filled his sails, he found still another land with lofty mountains and white peaks. This, too, when on approaching it he had found it an island, he passed by as useless. And now as the breeze grew strong, he ordered the sails to be partly furled; four days were passed on this part of the voyage; then at last a fourth time land was seen, which from the description of others he judged to be Greenland, and directing his ship towards it, he reached towards evening Cape Herjulfsnes, where his father lived; and having been more lucky in finishing his voyage, than he was wise in undertaking it, he ceased henceforth to travel and remained with his father as long as the latter lived, and after his death took possession of his estate.

CHAPTER II.

OF THE DISCOVERY OF VINLAND BY LEIF.

When Bjarne Herjulfson crossing over from Greenland came to Eric Hacon's son, the Earl of Norway, he was at first hospitably received by him and then enrolled in the number of his courtiers, and related what lands, until then untrodden by any one, as far as he knew, he had seen; in the opinion of the crowd, he was partly condemned, because he lacked ambition to explore them. The next summer he crossed to Greenland and there was repeatedly question of seeking those countries. To him, therefore, came Leif, the Lucky of Brattahlide, bought his ship and having hired thirty-five sailors, asked his father to become their leader for the purpose of looking up the lands recently seen. Eric excused himself on account of his old age, which made him less fit to bear the hardships of sea and tempest than he was in his youth. At last he yielded to the importunities of his son, and trusted to fortune which had favored him beyond the rest of his family; but setting out from home, when not far from the ship, he was thrown off his horse, which had grown restive, and sprained his foot; regarding this as an unfavorable omen he declared that fate had not ordained that he should discover more lands than the one they inhabited, and returned home, whilst Leif with his associates carried out their plans; among these there is said to have been a certain southerner (for by his name our ancient writers understand the Germans), Tyrker by name. The country last seen by Bjarne, first met their view, and approaching it, they sent out a boat; climbing up mountains covered by perpetual snow, they noticed that below as far as the sea, the land was covered with continuous rock, and was therefore utterly uninhabitable. Then said Leif: Bjarne's listlessness, at least, we have made amends for by exploring the country. I shall therefore, give it a name to match its character, and it shall be called HELLULAND, that is to say, rocky land. Starting thence they found another land; landing here, likewise, they found it flat, and without harbors, here and there green with woods, and again covered with white sand. This Leif called MARKLAND from its flatness (hence it is clear that the word MARK means not as some say "country," but "plain" or "flat land.") Sailing thence after a short delay, a north-wind filling their sails for two days; they again saw land, along whose northern side stretched an island. They brought their ship close up to this and disembarking in clear weather, they observed grass dripping with dew and vying even with honey in sweetness. Returning thence to their ship they brought it to the sound, which lay between the island and the cape, that stretched northward from the mainland: when sailing past the cape they veered towards the west, the water ebbed away, and the ship struck on the quick-sands, and was separated from the sea by great shallows. But so great was their eagerness to see the newly found land, that without waiting for the tide, they left the ship behind and immediately entered the land by a river which flowed from a lake; when the tide rose, they brought the ship by the river into the lake, and after fastening it by casting anchor they established huts on the bank and then built commodious winter quarters. Both river and lake abounded in great shoals of salmon, larger than any they had seen before. So great is the fertility of the soil and the mildness of the climate, that cattle did not seem to need hay in the winter season; there is no winter cold; the grass did not wither. In winter the days were longer than in Iceland or Greenland, the sun rose about nine o'clock at the time of the winter solstice and set at three o'clock. (That they were not very exact in this observation, is proved by the fertility of the country and the character of the climate; for nowhere else at 50° 26′, from the equator, where the longest day is eighteen hours and the shortest six, is such fertility known to prevail. For with them the parts of the day consisted of three hours; but they did not accurately distinguish them in these parts.) Then, their dwellings being completed, they were divided into two parties, some were kept home, others having drawn lots, were sent out to explore the country in a body, lest being scattered they be exposed to danger; but they were instructed not to explore it further than they could go and return in one day; Leif alternately joined each party, being everywhere welcome on account of his prudence and skill.

CHAPTER III.

OF THE DISCOVERY OF VINES AND WILD GRAPES, AND

OF LEIF'S RETURN.

Now it happened that when the exploring party returned, the German Tyrker alone was missing. Leif forthwith sent twelve men to seek him, for he was very anxious on his account, inasmuch as the man had lived a long time in his father's house, had been fond of himself from childhood and his devoted follower; they had not gone far from the winter quarters when they met him in a jolly frame of mind, and looking like a drunken man, who, rolling his eyes hither and thither, excited their laughter, being a man small of stature, but exceedingly skilled in all kind of mechanical arts. Asked for the reason of his delay and chattering for a long time in

German, a language unknown to the rest, he finally answered that he had gone a little further than Leif and found vines and grapes; when they expressed doubts, he assured them that he had been born where grapes grew in plenty. Therefore, dividing the work among his sailors, Leif set some to gather grapes and others to cut vines, and filled the boat with the former and the ship with the latter. The fields there produced wheat of their own accord, and the trees called MAUSUR; of each they took some to carry home, and some timbers of such size that they could be used to build houses. Leaving the newly found country in the beginning of spring, Leif called it, from the vines and grapes, Vinland or Wine Land. Then returning to Greenland with favorable winds, when its snow-clad mountains were in sight, he turned his ship from the straight course: when one of the crew asked the reason, whether he noticed a cliff or a ship, he answered that he was not clear about it. When all thought the object seen to be a cliff, he saw also some men wandering on them, for he was keener sighted than all the rest. But when they had all seen the shipwrecked men, he declared that if they were peaceful, he would take them out of danger, but otherwise he would bring them under his power; having despatched a smaller boat, he took off fifteen, together with their Norse captain Thorer, and received all, together with as much merchandise as they could take, into his ship, and brought them to the bay of Eriksfjord and to his paternal estate Brattahlide. Thorer with his wife Gudrid, Thorbjorn's daughter, and three sailors, he himself entertained; the rest he distributed among his neighbors, who gave them hospitality. Thereafter he received the name of the Lucky or Fortunate; this however, the manuscript Chronicle as well as the Codex Flateyensis, on page 233, contradicting itself, referred to the year 1000. Henceforth he is reported to have grown in wealth and reputation. But to his brother Thorvald the new country did not seem to have been sufficiently explored. Therefore he borrowed his brother's ship, on condition however, that he should first bring home the timber which Thorer's wrecked ship had carried, and which had been left on the cliff. The same winter disease breaking out among Thorer's crew, carried him off, with a great part of the men: Eric the Red, a man famed for discovering Greenland, died the same year. I cannot find the exact year either of the Christian era or of the reign of Yarls Eric and Sven who at that time ruled Norway.

CHAPTER IV.

OF THE VOYAGE OF THORVALD TO VINLAND AND HIS EXPLORATION OF PART OF IT; OF THE FINDING OF SOME PERSONS OF UNKNOWN RACE; OF THE SLAYING OF THORVALD, AND THE RETURN OF HIS COMPANIONS TO THEIR NATIVE COUNTRY.

Thorvald, having engaged thirty sailors, started off to Vinland and spent the winter in fishing, in the winter quarters of his brother Leif. The following spring, keeping back a light boat, he put a part of the sailors on board the ship and sent them to explore the western parts of the country, throughout the summer. The land seemed pleasant, being covered with woods that were at a short distance from the sea; the shore was covered with white sand, lined everywhere with many islands, separated from one another by extensive shoals: no human dwellings were found there, nay not even the dens of wild beasts: only in an island towards the west, wooden structures were found, pyramid-shaped, such as are used instead of barns, to store corn (the Codex Flateyensis calls them KORNHIALM AF TRE), but no other traces of man. And so they returned the same autumn to their winter quarters. The following summer the ship steering towards the eastern and northern shores was overtaken by storms and running on a headland, broke its keel and underwent repairs there for a long time. Hence Thorvald called the headland KIALARNES, that is to say, Cape Hull.

Then turning eastward they came to the entrance of a bay and steering the ship to the nearest headland, all covered with forests, brought her to a harbor. Then Thorvald, with all his crew, landed on the cape and was taken by the beauty of the spot: "Here," said he, "it is beautiful, and I should like to fix my home." And returning to the ship they beheld three hills on the sand below the headland: on betaking themselves thither they noticed three boats of leather or hide, and under each boat three men, one of whom escaped with his boat: the remaining eight were seized and slain, with great thoughtlessness, for it would surely have been better to humor them rather than frighten and exasperate them. Returning thence to the headland they saw within the bay some hills which they judged to be inhabited. Then a sudden sleep fell upon them all, so deep that it could not be shaken off even for the appointed watches; it was broken by a voice suddenly heard which called out as follows: "Awake, Thorvald, I beseech thee, with all thy companions, if you intend to save your lives: embark all of you with the greatest speed and depart hence." Aroused by these words, they behold the entire bay covered with boats; Thorvald, therefore, advises his men in this sudden emergency, to protect themselves by defences, made up of twigs and logs, but not to be forward in attacking the enemy. Then there arose a great crowd and poured upon them javelins and arrows right and left; but after a short hour they scattered in flight and disorder. These men the Norsemen called SKRAELINGS, in contempt, that is to say, DWARFS. Then Thorvald asked his men whether any of them had been wounded; when they told him that no one was hurt, he said, that he himself had been wounded, having been struck by a missile, which passing his shield, had lodged underneath the armpit, and that the wound no doubt was mortal; he therefore ordered himself to be carried to the headland, where he had intended to settle and bade them bury him there; adding that his intentions had not been frustrated, for that he would dwell there for a long time. He commanded two crosses to be erected, one at his head, the other at his feet, and the headland in future to be called KROSSANES, or "the headland of the crosses," and he ordered the men to hasten thence speedily. Here the Codex Flateyensis states, that at this time Greenland was converted to Christianity, though Eric the Red died before its conversion, whilst on page 233, it (the Cod. Flat.) stated, that in consequence of Leif's exhortations, Eric, with the whole population of Greenland had been baptized. There (at Krossans) Thorvald was buried, as he had instructed his men; but the sailors having returned to their companions, remained there the following winter. But in the ensuing spring, having laden their ship with vines and grapes, they weighed anchor and came to Greenland, to Leif, on the estate of Brattalihde.

CHAPTER V.

OF THE TOILSOME AND FRUITLESS VOYAGE OF LEIF'S BROTHER THORSTEIN, WHO INTENDED TO VISIT VINLAND; OF HIS FORCED RETURN TO GREENLAND WHEN THE PLAGUE HAD BROKEN OUT; OF HIS DEATH AND THE PRODIGY CONNECTED WITH IT.

Whilst these events took place in Vinland, Thorstein the third son of Eric the Red, married Gudrid, the wife of the Thorer, whom Leif had saved when Thorer was shipwrecked. Having now learned of his brother's death, he resolved to sail over to Vinland, in order to bring home Thorvald's remains. In the same ship, therefore, in which his brother had sailed, he weighed anchor, having shipped a crew of 25 chosen men, and obtained the winter-quarters of his brother Leif, not as a present but for use; he took his wife, to share not only his couch but also his voyage. Having been tossed about by storms all summer, he was carried one week after the beginning of winter into the western bay of Greenland, called Lysufjord: there he distributed all his sailors in winter-quarters in the neighborhood, but he alone with his wife, being without quarters, remained in the ship for some days: finally at the invitation of a certain Thorstein, surnamed Surt, or the Black, who was the only man there, who with his wife, called Grimhilde, inhabited a house without family; he staid with him and considering the means of the master, was entertained, if not sumptuously, at least kindly. In the beginning of winter a disease attacking all Thorstein's sailors, carried off many of them; their bodies he placed in coffins and put on the ship, intending to take them to Eric's bay and bury them in the spring. At that time Christianity was new in Greenland, and Thorstein the Black and his wife Grimhilde had not yet adopted its doctrines. The woman, in size and strength was a match for the strongest man: at length the same plague attacked her as well as Thorstein Ericson, and they lay ill at the same time. But she having died first, according to the custom of the less wealthy in those places, was to be placed on a bier: but whilst her husband Thorstein was busy in procuring it, Grimhilde, in presence of Thorstein Ericson, who was ill at the same time and of his wife Gudrid, began to look for her shoes, intending to rise; but going back to bed as her husband returned, she struck it with a great thud; her husband with great exertion and difficulty carried her out and buried her. Afterwards Thorstein Ericson died. Now Thorstein, the owner of the farm, to console his (Thorstein Ericson's) widow, promised to take her to Eriksfjord, with the corpses of her husband and his companions, and to bring many to his house, lest she would waste away there through dulness. Meanwhile the dead Thorstein sitting up in bed said: "Where is Gudrid?" and he thrice repeated this question. She, dazed by this prodigy, asked her host whether she must answer, and was prevented by him from doing so. But he went up to the bed and took a seat near it; then he enquired what he (Thorstein Ericson) wished. The latter answered that though he had reached a beautiful place, he desired to comfort his wife and make known to her her future destinies; he foretold that she would marry an Icelander, would live with him in his country for a long time, and that from him would spring a noble family; that she would visit Rome, would become a nun, near the church which was building in Iceland, and would peacefully die there in advanced old age. Whether this story be true, or was concocted and corrupted to flatter the bishops who were descended from her, I leave to the reader's judgment. After saying this Thorstein sank back into his bed. His corpse and those of his companions the other Thorstein honestly took where he had promised to bury them, and selling his farm emigrated with all his property to Ericsfiord, and lived there, but much more respected than before. The corpses were all buried near the Church, which had then been built; but Gudrid departed to her husband's brother, Leif.

CHAPTER VI.

OF THE VOYAGE OF KARLSEFNE TO VINLAND; OF HIS TRAFFIC WITH THE SKRAELINGS, AND OF THE DISPUTES THENCE ARISING, WHICH RESULTED IN OPEN WAR.

In the same year a very wealthy man, Thorfinn, surnamed Karlsefne, an Icelander, son of Thord of Hesthofde, grandson of Snorre by Thorhilde Riupa, daughter of Thord Geller, great grandson of Thord, of the estate Hofde, called also Spakonufellzhofde, starting from Norway to Greenland was hospitably received by Leif, and having gained his consent married Gudrid. He, with sixty sailors formed a partnership to colonize Vinland, the profits to be shared equally. Karlsefne was accompanied by his wife, took with him various kinds of animals, crossed over to settle Vinland and arrived in safety near Leif's tents, which he had received for a loan; there he found stranded on the coast a whale, of the species called REID, and considered one of the largest (being 100 and sometimes even 130 cubits long). This was a matter of much importance for their household stock; but the small and large cattle, and among them a fine bull, having found rich pasture, began to thrive greatly. Then Karlsefne ordered trees to be cut down and polished, and then to be placed on the rocks and dried. And they harvested all the products of the earth and sea, now gathering grapes and again fishing; (I am less convinced of what Bjorn of Skarzda, a distinguished Icelandish historian, inserted into his history, and which was no doubt copied from an ancient manuscript, that wheat grew there.) When the first winter was past and the summer had come, they saw the dwarfs, whom they called Skraelings, rushing in great numbers from the woods, not far from the place where the bull was grazing with the cows; frightened at his dreadful lowing the Skraelings turned to the house of Karlsefne, with their packs, which were filled with various kinds of furs, especially of the sable and of white mice. When they were about to enter at once by the door, they were kept back by the orders of the owner, who differed from them not only in bodily appearance, but also in language; nevertheless, putting down their packs, they exposed their goods for sale, wishing to exchange them for arms, which Karlsefne forbade as dangerous to himself and his men; instead of them he commanded the women to offer them food and refreshments, prepared from milk; having tasted these, they desired only them and nothing else and bartering food for their merchandise, they departed, gorged with food. Meanwhile Karlsefne repeatedly fortified his wooden structures. But in the beginning of winter when his wife had brought forth his son Snorre, the Skraelings returned in much greater numbers than before, provided as on the former occasion with wallets; again milk preparations were given them and paid for with packs thrown over the fences. Perchance Gudrid, who was seated in the house near the infant's cradle, remarked a shadow in the entrance: then a woman attired in a great black cloak, her head covered with linen, dark haired, pale faced, and with eyes of unusual size, too large for one head, entered and approaching addressed her in these words: "What is your name?" Having given it and asked the woman's name in return, she learned that she too was named Gudrid: but when she invited her to be seated, a great sound and noise was heard outside, for one of Karlsefne's servants killed one of the Skraelings, who was about to steal some arms, and immediately the woman, who had been seen by Gudrid alone and by no one else, disappeared. The Skraelings also, betaking themselves to flight, left behind them their wares and their garments. But Karlsefne, thinking that they would return in greater numbers, to avenge the death of their countryman, sent all his men to clear the interior of the woods, that the cattle might the more readily be concealed there, and he ordered ten men to show themselves on the headland, to entice the Skraelings more easily; for the battle-field he selected a spot between the wood and the water, lest his force be surrounded by numbers: the bull was placed before the line of battle. Nor was he mistaken; for the Skraelings flocked thither in great numbers, to their marked loss, for many were slain in the conflict. The bull too which was strange to them, greatly frightened them by his lowing, which was unpleasant to their ears. Among them one man, handsome in build, taller than the rest, was conspicuous and seemed to be the chief. When perchance one of the Skraelings, after seizing an axe that was lying by and looking at it for a while struck it into the head of a comrade and killed him by the blow, the tall man seeing this took it into his hands and examining it for a short time hurled it very far into the sea, seemingly detesting the iron that was forged to slay men. Immediately thereafter, all fleeing in disorder hid in the woods; but Karlsefne after passing the winter, the next spring loaded his ship with vines and other products that grew there, and returning to Greenland, reached the bay of Ericsfjord and wintered there.

CHAPTER VII.

OF THE FOURTH EXPEDITION TO VINLAND UNDER THE LEADERSHIP OF THORVARD, THE HUSBAND OF FREYDIS, AND TWO ICELANDERS, HELGE AND FIMBOG, OF THE INHUMAN CRUELTY OF FREYDIS AND OF KARLSEFNE'S RETURN TO ICELAND, AND OF HIS DESCENDANTS.

In the very summer that Karlsefne returned to Greenland, two brothers, born in the eastern district of Iceland, landed there from Norway and wintered there. Meantime Freydis, the daughter of Eric the Red, (a bastard according to Bjorn of Skardza), considering at Gardar the plan of revisiting Vinland in the following spring, went to them and invited them to join her in partnership; this was agreed upon with a fixed apportionment of gain and loss, the condition being added that the members of both parties should be equal and consist of thirty men only, fit for bearing arms, besides the women. Then she, having borrowed her brother Leif's tents, immediately broke the agreement about the number of the sailors, embarked five more men on her ship and concealed them until they had reached Vinland. The brothers, who had reached Vinland a little sooner, were bringing their effects into Leif's tent, which she on her arrival indignantly declared to be against the agreement, because it (the tent) had been loaned to her, not to them. They retorted that, an agreement having been made for the common advantage, they had supposed that the use of the tent also was common; nevertheless they declared that they would give way to her frenzy; for that they would not contend with her malice; and taking away their effects, they built another house on the shore. Now she ordered trees to be cut, vines perhaps (for so they are called in the account of the departure), with which she intended to load the ship. At the approach of winter the customary games were begun, but quarrels arising the games did not last long, all intercourse between the brothers and Freydis and her sailors, being for a long time broken off. On a certain morning Freydis, rising from bed without shoes, having put on only her husband's over-garment and having walked unaccompanied to the brothers' tents over the dew-covered ground, stood silent for a while in the doorway, which a sailor who had just gone out had opened; when Fimbog, who alone was awake, remarked this, he asked what was the matter. She called him out to a private conference and led him to a block of wood placed at the side of the tent for use as a bench and there they sat down. Then in answer to her question, how he was pleased there, he replied that he liked the land very well, but that their quarrels without any previous cause displeased him greatly; when she had declared that she too was displeased for the same reason, she stated the cause of her coming: for as she intended to return to Greenland, she said, she wished to exchange her ship for his as being larger, and he promised to give it to her, to please her. After this conversation they parted, Fimbog returning to his bed, she to her husband's. When the latter felt her feet, chill with cold and dripping with moisture, he asked the reason. She, seething with grief and rage, mingled reproaches with wailing, complaining that having gone out to the brothers' tents and asked for an exchange of ships, she had been overwhelmed with blows and covered with lashes, and saying that on account of his listlessness she would be exposed to the insults of all in the future, for that he had not the spirit to avenge her; therefore she had good reason to be homesick after her own country, where owing to the protection of her own family, she had always been and would thereafter be free from every insult and safe; moreover she threatened that if he delayed avenging this most foul insult, she would dissolve her marriage with him. Having embittered her husband by these and similar words, she suddenly stirred him up to call out all his men forthwith to take arms; entering the huts of the other party who were asleep, they bound them, led them forth, and beheaded them. All the men being slain, when the women only (they were five in number) remained and no one wished to slay them, she herself demanded an axe and killed them all with her own hand. Whilst all loathed her deed, she appeared as if triumphing over some exploit, threatened them one by one with death, if they made the matter known in Greenland, and ordered them to say, that the men who had been slain, were living in Vinland. On the approach of spring, she loaded the ship of which she had robbed the brothers with the products of Vinland and prepared it for her return to Greenland; they arrived there in the beginning of summer, while Karlsefne, in the bay of Eriksfiord, was waiting for favorable winds with a well equipped ship, the best that had left Greenland up to that time. But when she (Freydis) felt that the murders could not be kept hidden by fear and threats only, she generously divided the booty among her companions, and moreover bribed every one of them with gifts, because, besides the shame of their infamous gains and the fear of punishment, for they had all a share in the crime, the obligation incurred by accepting her gifts would more efficiently prevent their making known her misdeeds. Trusting to these wily expedients, she staid at home secure and quite wealthy, with her husband, Thorvard by name, who was subject to her orders. But not even so could the dreadful crime be kept concealed, without its being made known to her brother Leif, by the very men who had obeyed her in perpetrating it; he having examined three of them drew out the truth, and cursing his sister, declared that, though he did not wish to put her to death, he prophesied that her offspring would be unlucky. Thereafter Freydis, hated by all as long as she lived, passed a life infamous and devoid of all respect. Karlsefne, having weighed anchor with his wife Gudrid after a prosperous voyage reached Norway, plentifully provided with means; he was greatly honored by the chief men of that country and passed the winter there. But when his ship lay in port ready to sail to Iceland, a certain man of Bremen offered to buy its cornice (it is called HUSASNOTRA) for a quarter of a pound of gold: when he had sold it, he saw that it was made of the wood called MAUSR, previously unknown to him, although brought from Vinland.

(Arngrim thinks that the wood was the MAFHOLTERBAUM, or butcher's broom, (MEUSDORN) which, when used as a binding keeps off the mice, how correctly I know not; that this kind of wood was very precious appears from the life of Harold the Haughty, who presented a drinking bowl (of this wood) as a magnificent gift to Thorer of Steige who called it the Royal Cup. When he had afterwards arrived at the bay in Eastern Greenland called Skagafjord, and there passed the winter he bought the estate of Glaumba, and erected a building that was magnificent considering the place, and dwelt there: as long as he lived he was respected among the foremost men, and from him thereafter sprang a famous line. After his death his wife, after long presiding over the house, with her son Snorre, born in Vinland, went to Rome. On her return thence she learned that he, (Snorre) had built a church at home. Free from worldly cares henceforth, she devoted herself to God, having become a nun, and to the end of her life worked for holier ends. Snorre's son Thorgeir was the father of Ingveld, the mother of Bishop Brand, and Snorre's daughter Hallfrid was the mother of Runoff, the father of Bishop Thorlak. Snorre's own brother was Bjorn, the father of Thoruna, who begot Bishop Bjarne. Now what has been here related, as the Cod. Flat. page 288, declares, was copied down from the lips of Karlsefne. But it differs greatly from the story followed by Bjorn of Skardza, although the latter is redolent of the spirit of antiquity, and interspersed with very ancient verses, which Hauk, the judge (lagmare, nomophylax) collected: he flourished in 1406; it will be worth while to give a summary of this version.

CHAPTER VIII.

OF LEIF'S JOURNEY TO NORWAY TO KING OLAF TRYGGVESON; OF HIS DISCOVERY OF VINLAND ON HIS RETURN, AND OF HIS SUCCESSFUL PREACHING OF THE CHRISTIAN RELIGION IN HIS NATIVE COUNTRY.

He, Hauk, calls the wife of Eric the Red Thorhilde, and their sons Thorstein and Leif, uncommon men, of whom the former always remained with his father; and never was there in Greenland any man who excelled him in endowments of mind and body. Leif, on the contrary, he tells us, sailed away from Greenland, and first came to the Hebrides; there, having tarried a long time in summer, he kept company with Thorgunna, a woman of noble descent, but skilled in occult arts, or rather a sorceress. When she wished to accompany him, as he was leaving, Leif is reported to have asked whether this could be done with the consent of her relatives. She replied that she did not care for this; whereupon he replied, that with so small a retinue, he could not carry off so noble a lady. She declared that she was pregnant by him and would undoubtedly give birth to a son, whom she promised or threatened to send to him, as soon as his years would permit, saying that she would follow herself; moreover she foretold, that this son would one day be no more useful to him, than his departure at that time was agreeable to her. And Leif departing presented her a finger-ring as well as a cloak of Greenland stuff, and a belt adorned with animal's teeth. That boy, called Thorgils, subsequently came to Greenland and Leif recognized him as his son. He is also said to have come to Iceland in the summer, which preceded the prodigies of Froda (which cannot at all be correct, for these, according to the Eyrbyggva Saga, fall in the year of our Lord one thousand, which is the year in which the boy was born.) Having thereafter lived in Greenland, he is said before his death, to have seemingly performed some prodigy. What this was, I find nowhere explained more in full.

Leif sailing in autumn from the Hebrides to Norway, was held in high honor by King Olaf Tryggveson, and was commissioned by him to plant the Christian Religion in his native country in the following summer; for Leif is said to have been regarded by the King as a remarkable and a lucky man. On that voyage, going astray for a long time from the right course, he is said to have come upon unknown lands, in a situation where no one before had suspected that there was land. The soil spontaneously produced wheat; vines also grew there as well as the trees called MAUSR: now those trees are said to have been so large, that timbers fit for house-building were taken from them. On that voyage, it is related, he rescued a shipwrecked man, and on his return he made known the Christian Religion and exhibited letters of King Olaf, sure proofs of his royal will, and published the glories of the new faith in many words. His father, (Eric the Red) refused to embrace it, but his (Eric's) wife Thorhilde immediately accepted it and had a church built, where she with those who were converted, devoted herself to prayer. Afterward that church was called Thorhilde's Church. Having become a Christian she separated from her husband's bed and board, at which the latter was vexed. In the following winter Leif converted fifty Reppas or villages to Christ: Bjorn of Skardza relates that this event took place in the eastern district of the country.

CHAPTER IX.

OF THE FRUITLESS ATTEMPT OF LEIF'S BROTHER THORSTEIN TO EXPLORE VINLAND; OF HIS RETURN TO GREENLAND; OF HIS MARRIAGE WITH THORBJORN'S DAUGHTER GUDRID, OF HER EDUCATION AND AN-
CESTORS IN ICELAND.

Afterwards several Greenlanders were seized by the desire to explore the country found by Leif, the chief of whom was Thorstein Ericson, a wise and popular man. However the eyes of all were turned to Eric to be the leader of the expedition, for he was a lucky man as his discovery of Greenland proved and moreover distinguished by his experience: after long refusing he finally yielded to the requests of his friends. The ship of Thorbjorn Vifillson, (of whom more hereafter) was selected for the purpose and fitted out with twenty sailors and scant provisions. Early on a certain morning Eric rode away from home and first hid a box full of gold and silver; but on his way he fell from his horse, broke two ribs and severely injured his arm where it joined the shoulder. He therefore bade his wife Thorhilde to raise the hidden treasure, for he owned that he had met with the accident as a punishment for hiding it. Then they sailed from Ericsfjord amid great joy; but for a long time and wearily they strayed from their course, for they had Iceland in sight and also saw Irish birds; after being driven across the ocean they again arrived at the bay of Ericsfjord towards winter, and all the sailors, who had no homes, were liberally supported by Eric the Red during winter. In the same winter Thorstein, the son of Eric the Red, with the consent of his father married Gudrid, the daughter of Thorbjorn Vifillson: of her parents and her education as a girl a short account must be given. Vifill, the father of this Thorbjorn, was one of the companions of Queen Audr, an immensely rich woman, the mother of Thorstein the Red, and in fact Vifill was sold into slavery among the Irish captives before Audr restored him to freedom. But when she divided estates among her nautical followers and had passed him by, he is said to have asked why she did so; but she answered that it did not matter, for that wherever he would be, he would be a great man. However she gave him a valley called after his name Vifilsdal, where he afterwards dwelt to the end of his life. His sons were Thorgeir and Thorbjorn; they married the daughters of Einar of Laugabrekka, the son of Sigmund, the grandson of Ketil, Thistel, who gave his name to a bay, (Thistilsfjord): the former married Arnora, the latter Hallveiga, by whom Thorbjorn begat the above-mentioned Gudrid, of whom we are speaking, a maiden of wonderful beauty; her Orm, a wealthy man, of the estate of Arnestap, in the western quarter of Iceland, and his wife Halldise brought up. Her hand was refused to a certain Einar, in spite of his wealth, which he had made by trading, merely because he was born of a freedman, though the girl's father Thorbjorn, greatly needed means to support the expenses of his family. When Thorbjorn saw that his means were reduced, and his family could not be maintained with the same splendor as before, he preferred to plough the soil rather than give up his accustomed magnificence. He therefore departed to Greenland to his friend Eric the Red, whom he had helped in Iceland with money and men. For when Eric left Iceland he promised his friends that he would not fail to help them in need, if the occasion to do so should ever present itself. With thirty sailors and among the number Orm and his wife and family, who could not bear to desert him, Thorbjorn left his country and was borne to Cape Herjulfsnes, and there hospitably received and generously supported with all his sailors, by a wealthy man, the foremost of the place, Thorkel by name. But a sickness arose on the voyage and spread among the sailors, and Orm, as well as his wife, was carried off thereby.

CHAPTER X.

OF A CERTAIN PROPHETIC WOMAN; OF HER APPEARANCE AND OF HER SKILL IN THE MAGIC (SEIDIC) ART.

At that time a dreadful famine afflicted Greenland and many desired to know how long it would last and hoped that they would easily find this out during the winter, from a certain prophetic woman, Thorbjorg by name. She was wont to stop in that country with those who, eager to know the future and their own fortunes, invited her to stay with them. But as Thorkel was looked upon as by far the most prominent man of the district, it seemed incumbent on him to take this burden upon himself and satisfy the wishes of the people. Thorkel therefore invited her to his home, and, as usual, treated the woman with respect; she was the sole survivor of nine sisters, all prophetesses. A lofty seat on a platform was prepared for her and a pillow filled with cock's feathers placed under her; the appearance of the wise woman is described as follows: She put on a dark blue cloak tied with thongs (they call them TINGLA MOTTUL) adorned down to its lowest border with little stones; around her neck hung little glass balls; on her head she wore drawn up a cowl of black lambskins and white catskins; in her hand she carried a staff, crowned with a brass globe studded with little stones; she wore a girdle (Thomas Barthol translates "HUNLANDICD" according to the words of the copy, which he followed; this reads HYNDSKAN LINDA; mine reads HNIOSKU LINDA. i. e. 'dry girdle or zone' which makes no sense: I conjecture that it should be written HUNDSKINS LINDA, i. e., 'a dogskin girdle,' for the various other skins suggest this selection;) from it hung an immense pouch, in which were stowed the instruments of her magic art; to her feet she attached shaggy calfskin shoes with long latchets, at the ends of which were large tin balls: on her hands she wore catskin gloves, shaggy and white on the inside. All saluted her respectfully, but she received their greetings, according as she favored them. Thorkel having taken her hand led her to the seat prepared for her, and begged her to look at his house, family, flocks and herds with care; but she in reply to most of his remarks was silent. The dishes served to her were porridge of goat's milk, and the hearts of all the kinds of animals that were found there; she used a brass spoon, a knife with its point broken off, whose handle was made of whale's teeth, and which was encircled by two brass bands. When the meal was ended, the tables were removed. Thorkel went up to her, asking whether she had had an open view, how she was pleased with the house and the ways and dispositions of its inmates, and how soon she could know, what was to be investigated. She answered that she could give no reply, till she had slept there a night. On the following afternoon, all things necessary for magic (seidic) incantations were furnished. But first of all she asked for women, who knew a song called VARDLOKR, which was absolutely necessary to practice the Seidic art; but no one was found that knew it. Then Gudrid, Thorbjorn's daughter, answered: "I am not a sorceress and know nothing of the magic art; however Halldise, my teacher in Iceland taught me a song called VARDLOKR," "Indeed" said Thorkel, "you are blessed for your knowledge." Then Gudrid replied: "Magic is the only thing I will in no wise abet; for I am a Christian." From this remark, compared with what has been said above, it follows that Vinland was discovered after the year 1000. But the wise woman suggested that she could oblige her friends without offense to her religion. Overcome by this temptation of Satan, the tender maiden sang a magical song with a sweet melody to the admiration of all: meanwhile the women stood around the platform on which the sorceress sat. The song being ended the sorceress thanked Gudrid, saying that many and various spirits, who were before about to leave and refused to obey her, allured by the song and the sweet notes of the songstress had approached, and that many things that were before concealed, had become manifest to her. She foretold to Thorkel that the corn famine would not last beyond winter and that it would be relieved when the weather would grow mild, that the disease which had thus far harrassed them would cease faster than they thought; that she would recompense Gudrid for the aid given her, that she (Gudrid) would soon marry the greatest man in Greenland, that the marriage would not last long however, as the fates recalled her to Iceland, that there a great and distinguished offspring would be born of her, which was illumined by brighter rays than she could bear to look upon; having then saluted Gudrid in a friendly way she dismissed her. Afterwards persons, who wished to know certain matters, consulted her, each for himself; and she, freely answering the questions, unravelled what she was asked. Then she was called by messengers to other estates: on her departure, Thorbjorn, Gudrid's father, who had refused to be present at the impious ceremonies and the magic rite and had gone to another estate, was recalled. The words of the witch were verified in every respect, for both the famine and the death ceased on the approach of spring, as well as the plague that had begun with Thorbjorn's sailors. Thorbjorn, therefore, taking his vessel from Cape Herjulfsnes, came to the bay of Ericsfjord and when his arrival had been celebrated with great joy by Eric, was entertained hospitably with all his family during all the winter or rather during the rest of the winter, (for the ancients reckoned the early part of spring as winter); but the following spring Eric pointed out to Thorbjorn some land in Stockanes, where he built quite a roomy house and laid out a magnificent estate, where he dwelt as long as he lived. Then Thorstein, the son of Eric the Red, married Gudrid with Thorbjorn's consent; the Codex Flateyensis says, that she married Thorstein, as a widow, having previously been married to Thorer whom Leif saved when shipwrecked. The nuptials were celebrated with great pomp at Brattahlide, during Eric's lifetime, contrary to the report of the Codex Flateyensis.

CHAPTER XI.

OF THE INFECTIOUS DISEASE THAT AROSE AMONG THORSTEIN'S CREW; OF HIS DEATH AND A PRODIGY, AND OF THE ANCIENT MODE OF BURIAL IN GREENLAND; OF THE ARRIVAL OF KARLSEFNE AND HIS MARRIAGE TO GUDRID.

The half of the estate called Lisufjord (I should prefer to read "of a certain estate in Lisufjord") Thorstein owned, the other half a namesake, who had also a wife, named Sigrid (Grimhild in the Cod. Flat.) Thither Thorstein, the son of Eric the Red, betook himself with his wife, at the beginning of autumn, and there he passed the winter; but an infectious disease invaded the entire house. A steward named Gard, a man disliked by many, fell a victim and then the rest, and finally the plague seized Thorstein Ericson also, and Sigrid the other Thorstein's wife, and they lay ill at the same time. But Sigrid, who was ailing, accompanied by Thorstein Ericson's wife one evening retired to a privy where, the ailment increasing in violence, she was unable to repress her wails. Having heard her wails, Gudrid regretted that they had gone too far to be heard, when crying for help, and urged her to return in haste; Sigrid answered that she was stopped by ghosts, that were standing at the door and that among the number she recognized herself and Gudrid's husband Thorstein. After a while she advised that they return, for the ghosts had vanished; but she said that she saw Thorstein holding a scourge, about to lash the rest. After they had returned home, she died the same night and a coffin was prepared to bury her corpse. But as her husband Thorstein had taken some oarsmen to the harbor, who were about to go on a fishing expedition, he was hastily recalled by a messenger from the sick Thorstein, who feared danger from his (the other Thorstein's) wife Sigrid, lately deceased; she had risen from the dead and harassing him seemed to be about to get under his bed-clothes. Thorstein (Sigrid's husband) returned, and finding that she had entered Thorstein's bed buried a large axe in her breast. But Thorstein Ericson died towards nightfall. But when night had worn on a little, he raised himself and bade his wife Gudrid be called, declaring that this hour was allowed him by God to settle his affairs. The host, therefore, roused her from sleep, made known to her her husband's commands, and said, he did not know what to advise her in the matter. But she answered that this prodigy would be memorable that trusting to the Divine Mercy, which had always been kind to her, she would go to her husband and learn what he had to say; for, if any danger threatened, she would not escape it, nor would she be the cause why her deceased husband should wander about after death; that there was great reason to fear that this might happen, if she proved faithless to him. On approaching the dead man, it seemed to her, she saw him pouring forth tears; afterwards he whispered some words in her ear privately, known to her alone. But in public he spoke as follows : Blessed are they who embrace the Christian religion, for it is based on Divine grace and mercy: few however religiously observe it ; moreover, from the very establishment of religion in Greenland, the dead have been sinfully buried in unconsecrated ground, the funeral rites being scantily celebrated. He, so he continued, wished to be carried to church with the others who had died there, except Gard alone, because he had troubled those who had died thus far during the winter. That man, he warned them, ought to be burned as soon as possible in the avenging flames. Then he foretold some of his wife's future destinies and bade her to beware of marrying any Greenlander and to give her money to the Church, and partly also to the poor. Having said this he again fell asleep. A similar story is told in the seventh book of "Chronicles" by Dithmar of Merseburg. It was customary in Greenland, and in other half-christian or even uncivilized lands that were visited by ships, to bury the dead in unconsecrated ground, to place sticks over their breasts for the purpose of marking the grave of the buried man; after a lapse of time, however long, the priest pulled out the sticks, poured some water into the hole by way of lustration and performed burial songs. Thorstein was carried to the church along with the other dead. But Gudrid went to her husband's father, Eric the Red, who treated her as a daughter. Shortly after her father Thorbjorn of Stockanes died; as she was his sole heir, Eric took upon himself the whole care of her patrimony and administered it faithfully. At the same time two ships from Iceland came to the bay of Ericsfjord : the one was commanded by Thorfinn Karlsefne, accompanied by Snorre Thorbrandson, of the estate of Skogastrand on Alftafjord bay in Iceland, and forty sailors ; the other was commanded by Bjarne Grimolfson, from the district adjoining Breidafjord Bay, together with Thorhall Gamlason from the eastern part of the island, and carried as many sailors; (the Cod. Flateyensis says that Karlsefne came from Norway.) Now Eric the Red setting out

with several natives to trade with these was received kindly
and invited to take as a gift all he wished, of the goods for
sale. Unwilling to be outdone in generosity, he invited the
entire crews of both ships to his house to pass the winter,
and they, pleased with his generous hospitality, took all their
merchandise thither: and they found buildings large enough
to receive them and everything was furnished generously.
As Christmas approached, Eric grew sad. Karlsefne re-
marking this, asked the cause of this sudden change, promising to pay liberally for what Eric had with great generosity
spent on them. The latter replied that they were most welcome guests, inasmuch as they received what he offered
them with grateful hearts; but that he was not disposed to
cause loss to his friends; he regretted that when after
leaving him they would come to other lands, they might
justly complain, that nowhere did they rembember the
Christmas or Yule festival to have been celebrated more
scantily than at Brattahlide, in Greenland with Eric the
Red. Karlsefne saw that this trouble could be easily dispelled, for he had corn and barley in plenty to furnish the
banquet with all the generosity Eric wished, and he allowed
Eric to bring it home. Eric did this and nowhere is a more
splendid festival said to have been celebrated in a poor
country. At the end of the feast, Karlsefne spoke to Eric
of marrying his daughter-in-law Gudrid, for he was her
guardian, and easily obtained her hand; the wedding was
celebrated with great splendor at Brattahlide, and there the
winter was passed. And this is the story of Gudrid and
her parents; let us return to Vinland.

CHAPTER XII.

OF KARLSEFNE'S VOYAGE TO VINLAND AND OF HIS COMPANIONS ON THAT EXPEDITION, VIZ: BJARNE, THORHALL AND THORVARD, THE SON-IN-LAW OF ERIC THE RED, AND ERIC'S SON THORVALD.

During the same winter the conversation often turned upon a voyage to Vinland (according to these documents, however, Leif is not reported to have given it this name). In the beginning of spring Karlsefne and Snorre fitted out their ship for the expedition; Bjarne and Thorhall, whom we have mentioned before, embarking in their own ship, were taken as partners in the undertaking. A third ship was commanded by Thorvard, the son-in-law of Eric the Red, who had married his illegitimate daughter Freydis, and by Eric's son Thorvald, and these were accompanied by Thorhall surnamed the hunter. This man tall in stature, of great strength, gigantic build and dark complexion, rudely and sharply spoken and of gloomy and forbidding appearance, had long followed the family of Eric the Red and spent his summers in hunting and his winters as steward. This man always suggested dark plans to Eric, for he was careless in practising the Christian religion, but very well acquainted with pathless and desert places and solitudes. One hundred and forty, (but as has been often said, the hundred consisted of twelve tens) sailors took part in this expedition. They sailed in the first place to the western part of inhabited Greenland, thence to the Bjarney Islands, for a night and a day (TVO DAEGR), thence southwards, till land came in sight. There many large cliffs projected twelve cubits broad; there was also a large number of foxes; this land they called HELLULAND. Thence they sailed for a day and night toward the southeast by east, until they saw a wooded land abounding in animals; southeast by south of this main land lay an island. There they killed a bear and from this circumstance called the island Bjarney and the main land Markland:

thence they sailed southward until they reached a certain headland: there the hull of a ship was found and the cape was therefore called Kjalarnes and they named the shore FURDUSTRAND, or wonderful, or wonderfully vast strand. Then the land was indented with bays, and after entering one of these Karlsefne sent forth a man and woman of the Scotch race, so swift in running that they outran wild animals; these King Olaf Tryggvason had presented to Leif when departing. The man's name was Hake, the woman's Hekja. He gave them a night and two days to explore the land and ordered them to start southward; at the appointed time they returned, the one bearing a cluster of grapes, the other an ear of wheat. Their garment, called KIAPAL which was sleeveless and open at the sides, was at the same time a covering for the head, and a clasp fastened it between the thighs. Then setting sail they entered another bay, near whose entrance lay an island, surrounded by currents, and thence called Straumsey: there they wintered and landed their cattle. The land was very fertile but produced neither vines nor grain. Here forgetting the things necessary to support themselves during the winter, which must be collected in autumn, they occupied themselves in exploring the country. But in the island there was so great a number of the ducks, whose feathers are most prized and which are called by the Norse AERD or contracted AER, that they could hardly walk over it without destroying the eggs. But winter coming on and fishing and hunting being impossible, a dearth of provisions followed. They therefore prayed to God; but when their prayers were not heard as soon as they wished, Thorhall the hunter set out; after seeking him two days and a night, they at last found him lying on a steep ridge, with mouth wide open and murmuring something: to their questions, what he was doing there, he made no reply; however, he went home with them. Shortly after a sea-monster was cast on the shore, but no one knew what kind of fish it was; when they cooked and eat it, it seemed not to agree with them. Then said Thorhall, the Red one (he meant Thor) is after all more powerful than your Christ, for with this did he reward the song which I sang in his honor; for he has seldom failed me. Having learned this, they threw the fish into the sea and committed themselves and all they had to God. Soon the weather grew mild and the sea, now quiet, was fit for fishing; thenceforth they had enough of food by land and sea, for there was also abundance of game.

CHAPTER XIII.

OF THORHALL THE HUNTER, WHO IS DRIVEN BY STORMS TO IRELAND AND THERE HELD IN BONDAGE TO THE END OF HIS LIFE; OF THE FURTHER EXPLORATION OF VINLAND BY KARLSEFNE AND HIS COMPANIONS; OF THE LAND AND WATER PRODUCTS THERE; OF THE DRESS OF THE SKRAELINGS AND THEIR TRAFFIC, AND OF THE DISPUTES AND WARS THENCE ARISING, WHICH HOWEVER END IN THE SKRAELINGS SUSTAINING GREATER LOSS.

Thorhall the hunter, with nine sailors, passing Furdustrand with ship turned northward, sought Vinland. Two pieces of verse are extant, sung by him whilst he brought water into the ship, which have the true flavor of antiquity and in fact are marked by the genius of that age. Having doubled Kialarnes whilst he was sailing westward, a storm arising from the west drove him to Ireland, where he and his men passed a wretched existence, being kept in cruel bondage, until they were punished with death on account of their hatred of Christianity and their impiety. This story is reported to have been brought to Iceland by merchants. But Karlsefne with Snorre and Bjarne, sailing southward, in order to seek in the opposite direction, after a long voyage came to a place where a river rising in a marsh emptied into the sea; but his ship could not enter the river, because long estuaries intervened and the tide was running low: therefore they moored her at the mouth of the stream; there the level country produced wheat, the hills native vines; all the streams were full of fish, which, when ditches had been dug to the verge of the sea, so as to receive the tide water, were carried into these and caught with the hands whilst the tide lasted or receded; this kind of fish they called SACRED because they were caught without labor, I fancy. Many and various kinds of animals wandered over the fertile meadows and through the woods. After passing there two weeks spent in refreshing their bodies by sports without a sign of human cultivation appearing, they beheld one morning approaching them many boats covered with hides: in them javelins were raised as signals and whirled around, following the motion of the sun and creaking with the friction. Snorre Thorbrandson and Karlsefne interpreted them to be signs of peace and advised that they should, carry a white shield at their head and go to meet the strangers; when they saw this they rowed up vigorously and landed, wondering at the Greenlanders; nor did the latter wonder less at them, for they were swarthy, of ill-favored appearance, with short hair, broad cheek bones and large eyes; then after a short delay, having passed the headland, the strangers turned their boats southward. Thorfinn with his companions had passed a winter without snow, in huts, which he had erected in different places nearer to or farther away from the sea; the cattle feeding on grassy fields needed no other fodder. But in the beginning of spring, hide-covered boats, swarming in the bay, brought parties of Skraelings with signals of peace: they were received with white shields and induced to land. Then they bartered on the one side pieces of red cloth a span broad, with which the strangers were wonderfully pleased and which they wrapped about their heads, on the other side fur skins; when the red cloth proved insufficient to satisfy the wishes of those who asked for them, pieces of a finger's breadth were given them; Karlsefne's bull, perchance rushed out from the wood and so frightened them with its horrid bellowing, that they forthwith betook themselves to flight and staid away for three weeks. When these were passed an immense number of small skiffs arrived and seemed almost to cover the whole sea; and they whirled their signals not as before, when they meant peace, in the direction of the sun's motion, but in the opposite direction. Karlsefne recognizing this as a declaration of war ordered a red shield to be raised and went to meet them with an armed force. But the Skraelings rushing out of their ships, assailed them at a distance with missiles hurled from slings, and then threw a dark blue ball, not unlike a sheep's stomach stuck on a spear, on the ground above Karlsefne's soldiers, but kept back the spear; this ball striking the earth with great noise, caused such dread and terror, that Karlsefne with his companions saw their only safety in flight. They rushed along the upper river bank in a disorderly manner and seemed to be surrounded on all sides, both on land and sea, by the numbers of the enemy; nor could their flight be stayed until they reached some steep rocks. There recovering their courage, they resisted bravely. But Freydis, seeing her countrymen fleeing, came up fearlessly and cried out: "How do you, warriors, flee from those dwarfs, whom you can slaughter like sheep: forsooth had I arms, I should hack them into pieces more boldly than any of you." Her words nowise encouraged the panic-stricken fugitives. Therefore, as she could not follow them, when they fled to the woods, (for she was pregnant) it seemed wholly unlikely that she would escape the Skraelings. While she was pursued by them she came upon the corpse of one of her countrymen; it was Thorbrand Snorreson, whose skull had been crushed with a stone. Having seized his sword, she prepared to fight. But when she saw several running up to her, she uncovered her breast and approached it to the sword. Frightened by this, the Skraelings fled to their boats and departed in great haste. Karlsefne, having praised Freydis, began to consider what men they were that had rushed forth from the woods; at last it was found that they were pure illusions, and that there were no forces except those which had been in the boats and attacked them. Then he took to bandaging the wounded. Two Norsemen were lost in that battle, but many Skraelings. One of the latter, when he had come upon the corpse of a Greenlander and picked up his axe that lay next to him, struck it into a block of wood; but when the

Skraelings noticed that the axe was fit for cutting and sharp, one after the other tested its sharpness by cutting wood. But when one man made the same experiment on a stone, he broke the axe. Now when it was not found as fit to cut stone as wood, it was looked upon with scorn and thrown into the sea with a great effort. Karlsefne foreseeing that there would be constant danger from the natives, decided to abandon the land, however pleasant it might be. Intending therefore to return to Greenland, as he sailed northward, he came upon five sleeping Skraelings, dressed in garments of skins. Next to them lay hollow pieces of wood, like reeds, filled with animal marrow mixed with blood. Conjecturing by this sign that they had been driven into exile, the Norsemen killed them. Afterward they were borne to a headland so full of wild beasts, that it was almost entirely covered with their excrements, for there the beasts stopped over night. The Norsemen called it MIKIUNES from the manure. Thence they came to the bay of Straumsfjord, where plenty of all kinds of necessaries were found. Others relate that Karlsefne, together with Snorre, when he landed the first time at Straumsey, set sail southward from that harbor with one ship manned with forty sailors, for the purpose of seeking Vinland; that he left behind him the hundred others, including his wife and Bjarne; that not quite two months passed before their return and that he brought them thence to Vinland, where the winter was passed. Then Karlsefne, setting out with a single ship to find Thorhall the hunter, by sailing northward doubled Cape Kialarnes, and changing his course slightly towards the west, coasted along the land that lay on his left, which was an unbroken desert interrupted by no cultivated district, until entering the mouth of a river that flowed from east to west, he found a suitable harbor for his ship.

CHAPTER XIV.

OF THE SLAYING OF THORVALD, THE SON OF ERIC THE RED, BY A ONE-FOOTED BEING, OF KARLSEFNE'S SOJOURN AT STRAUMSFJORD FOR THREE WINTERS, OF THE BIRTH OF HIS SON SNORRE, OF THE CAPTIVITY OF TWO SKRAELINGS, OF THE DANGEROUS VOYAGE OF BJARNE GRIMOLFSON IN THE IRISH OCEAN, OF HIS HONORABLE CONDUCT TOWARD A CERTAIN ICELANDER IN EXTREME PERIL OF LIFE, OF KARLSEFNE'S RETURN TO ICELAND AND OF HIS DESCENDANTS.

One morning on the shore something was seen to move; when they had shouted at it, a one-footed being, rising up near the bank of the river, where the ship stood at anchor, rushed forth and immediately buried an arrow in the flank of Thorvald Ericson. When Thorvald had drawn it out and seen his own fat clinging to it, he said: "Fertile indeed is the land we have found, though we are hardly allowed to enjoy it." Shortly after he died of this wound, Karlsefne with his companions pursuing the unipede as he swiftly ran towards the north, at times had him in view, until he rushed headlong into a certain bay. This adventure one of them celebrated in a song, which exists to this day. Thence sailing northward they thought they saw the country of the unipedes and deemed it useless to run further risks. But the mountains that begin at the harbor in Vinland called Hoop, they found were continued in an uninterrupted range by the very mountains in the place where they were staying, and that in the middle was Straumsfjord, equidistant from there and from Hoop. Then they passed the first winter in Straumsfjord, (whither they seem to have been driven back by the winds) where a dangerous dispute arose about the common use of the women which the unmarried men claimed should be promiscuous. At the beginning of autumn Karlsefne's son Snorre, who had been born there and was now three years old, set sail from Vinland. Thence, their sails filled with the south wind, they came to Markland; here they found five Skraelings, one bearded, two women and as many boys; the rest got off and escaped into the earth (where perchance they had haunts;) but the boys were caught. Being afterwards brought away and taught the language of Greenland and made acquainted with Christian rites, they said that their mothers name was VETTHILDE, and their fathers name VAEGE. Two kings, they reported, ruled the Skraelings, one called AVALLDAINNA, the other VALLDIDIDA. Among them there were no houses, their place being supplied by caves and dens; facing their country was another, which was inhabited by men dressed in white garments, and terrible on account of the noise they made, before whom spears were born, from which hung cloths. It was believed that they described HVITRA MANNA LAND or White Man's Land, or HIBERNIA MAGNA. Bjarne Grimolfson was swept away by a tempest to the Irish Ocean. When the sea, which was full of worms, that gnawed and pierced the ship, foiled the efforts of the men that baled out the ship, and the water filled it, it began gradually to sink in the waves. They had a boat covered with a tar made from seal's grease: that kind of boats the worms never perforate (they are called SELTJORU.) As this could contain only one-half of the sailors and all had not the means of escaping, Bjarne ordered them to determine by lot, without regard for any one's rank, who were to go in the boat. No one opposed so fair a proposal. The lot favored him among others. As he entered the boat an Icelander, who by lot was left behind, cried out: "Will you abandon me here?" Bjarne said that it was done by the decision of the lot. "And yet," answered the other, "you promised my father in Iceland that we should share the same lot." "Be it so," answered Bjarne, since you cling so desperately to life, enter the boat, for I shall willingly yield you my place." And so returning to his ship he preferred to life faith and honor, the loss of which he dreaded much more than present death that stared him in the face. The skiff arrived safe with Bjarne's companions at Dublin, a celebrated city of Ireland. But Bjarne with the rest, all think, was swallowed up in the waves, for nothing further was heard of him. By what right he sacrificed his life, granted to him by God, I shall not discuss; but surely he left to all posterity a remarkable example of good faith, which he would by no means have imperilled, had he taken advantage of the favors of fortune. In the following summer Karlsefne is reported to have crossed to Iceland with his wife and to have betaken himself to his mother, on the estate of Reinarnes. Hauk, NOMOPHYLAX or chief judge of Iceland, about the year 1294, compiled the book of which the above are extracts, and which is called HAUK'S BOK or Hauk's book after his name, from the writings of the monk Gunnlaug, who died in the year 1219, and from several other old chronicles, both pagan and Christian. He enumerates his ancestors from Thorfinn Karlsefne, beyond the genealogy contained in the Codex Flateyensis, as follows: Karlsefne's son Snorre had a daughter Steinvor, the wife of Eniar of the manor of Grund, the grandson of Ketill, the great-grandson of Thorvald Krok, the great-great-grandson of Thorer, of the manor of Espishol. By her he begat a son Thorstein, called Ranglat, or the wicked, the father of Gudrun, the wife of Jorund, of the manor of Kelldum. Their daughter Halla bore Flose; the daughter of Flose, Valgerdis, was the mother of the chief judge Erlend the Strong, the father of our chief judge Hauk who is the ninth from Karlsefne. Another daughter of Flose, who was sixth from Karlsefne, was Thordis the mother of Ingibjorg, called the Rich, whose daughter was Hallbera, Abbess of the monastery of Reinenes. Many other distinguished families in Iceland are said to have been descended from Karlsefne and Gndrid. And this is the story the Antiquities relate of Vinland; many details, it is true, contradict one another; but I abstain from examining these.

CHAPTER XV.

ADAM OF BREMEN'S STORY OF VINLAND CONSISTENT WITH THE ABOVE; HIS GREAT MISTAKE REGARDING ITS POSITION; OLAF RUDBECK NO LESS ERRONEOUSLY IDENTIFIES VINLAND WITH FINLAND; THE STORY OF THE POSITION OF GREAT IRELAND; OF ARE THE ICELANDER AND THE PITCH OF THE GREENLANDERS.

"Moreover," says Adam of Bremen, he (*i. e.*, Sven Astritharson, King of Denmark) spoke of one other island found by many in that ocean, (which washes Norway and even Finnmark) an island called Winland, because vines grow wild there; that corn also abounds there without being sown, we have found to be proven, not by some storied opinion but by the undoubted history of the Danes." This statement compared with our narrative proves that the report about Vinland seemed at that time not idle, but to merit undoubting belief, because it was supported by the experience and testimony of reliable men; for Adam of Bremen lived at the time of Harold the Haughty, King of Norway. Now Harold began to reign in the forty-sixth or rather the forty-fifth year after Vinland was first discovered and afterwards settled. Concerning these events he adds to his recital: "Beyond this island (he has been speaking of Vinland) no other habitable land is found in that ocean; but all beyond is full of intolerable ice and unbounded darkness; this fact Marcianus mentions, saying that after one day's sail beyond Thyle the sea is frozen solid. This was lately tested by Harold, the most experienced chief of the Northmen; for having explored with ships the latitudes of the northern ocean, when the limits of the ceasing world were wrapt in darkness before his eyes, he escaped with difficulty the immense depth of the abyss by retracing his steps." Olaf Rudbeck, in chapter 7, paragraph 8, page 291 of his *Atlantica*, writes as follows on this passage: "Something like this no doubt had of old persuaded Adam of Bremen that in the extreme north, near the sea of ice, was situated an island that produced the vine, and was for that reason called Vinland. This he believed on the authority of the Danes, however, as he himself does not hesitate to state on page 37 of his work on the situation of Denmark; but that he was deceived either by the credulity of the Danes or by his own, is clearly shown by the similarity of the name of Finland, a province belonging to our kingdom, for which in Snorro and the History of the Kings the name of Vinland occurs more than once, and whose headland stretches into the extreme north and even to the sea of ice." He thinks that by Vinland Adam of Bremen understood Finland, and that he took the Finnish ale for wine, though that drink is common to the Fins and other northern nations and can hardly be mistaken for grapes and vines, which, Adam of Bremen thinks, grow wild in Vinland. And that he was not deceived by the Danes, as Rudbeck supposes, is plain from the facts we have stated. But where the name of Vinland occurs in Snorro and the Histories of the Kings, I have not up to this time found out.

Concerning the Great Ireland spoken of, which the ancients call White Man's Land, or Albania, the Origins of Iceland say, that it is separated from Ireland or Hibernia by a distance which you can measure by a six day's voyage towards the west, and they place it near Vinland. Thither, as the same book relates, Are Marson, the great-grandson of Ulf Skialg, who first settled the district of Reikjanes, in the western districts of Iceland, was driven by a storm: there he was first initiated into the mysteries of Christianity, and there although he was not allowed to depart, he was well treated and held in great honor. Hrafn, called the Limerick-trader, from his frequent voyages to Limerick, a city of Ireland, first brought this report to Iceland, and Thorkel Geiterson affirmed, that the same story was afterwards related in the Saga of Thorfinn, Earl of the Orkneys. This Are was the cousin of Thorhild (whom others call Thiodhild) the wife of

Eric the Red, who discovered Greenland. For Jorund, the other son of Ulf Skialg, and the brother of Mar by his wife Thorbjorg, called Knarrabringa, begat this Thorhild. The genealogy of Ulf Skialg we have traced from Hjorleif the Gallant, king of Hordia, as set down in his life. Pitch from seal's fat is said to be used by the Greenlanders alone; they hang up oil fried from seal's fat, and put it into boats of skin to dry, until it thickens, then color it black and besmear the ships. This method Bjorn of Skardza described; to me it seems more likely that it can be dissolved, unless something else be added to the seal's fat.

CHAPTER XVI.

OF THE VOYAGES OF THE SAXON BISHOP JONES, AND OF ERIC, BISHOP OF GREENLAND, TO VINLAND, AND OF GUDLEIF GUDLAUGSON.

The appendix to the Landnama Book relates that Jones or Johannes, a Saxon Bishop, (the Hungrvaka book, which is written on the history of the bishops of Iceland, asserts that he was an Irishman, or Hibernian,) after first preaching the Christian faith for four years in Iceland, set out thence for Vinland, in order to convert its people, and finally sealed his mission there by suffering torture and death.

In the year 1121, Eric, bishop of Greenland, visited Vinland. His family, the book on the Origins of Iceland, part 1, On the general occupation, chapter 13, page 15, traces back to the first settlers of Iceland. Eric's father being Gnup, Gnup's Birning, Birning's Gnup, Gnup's Grimkel, Grimkel's Bjorn, surnamed Gullbera or Gold-bearer, who first settled southern Reykjadal, a district of Southern Iceland. Grimkel's wife was Signya, Valthiof's daughter, who occupied the whole district called Kios; his father was Aurlig, who occupied a great part of Kjalarnes; his father was Hrap, the son of Ketill Flat-nesi or Flat-nose, the grandson of Bjorn Buna.

I know not whether this Vinland or some other uncertain part of America is meant by the land, to which, as the Eyrbyggja Saga reports, Gudleif Gunnlaugson of the province of Straumfjord in the western district of Iceland, sailing from Dublin, a city of Ireland, towards the end of St. Olaf's life, was driven on his return to Iceland by east and north winds. On this occasion he fell into great danger of death or of lifelong slavery, after losing his way and roaming for a long time over the western ocean without meeting any land. But then an extensive country which they saw, attracted the sailors, who were worn out with hardships and weak with long seasickness, to a safe harbor by the hope of refreshment. When they had reached shore, the inhabitants started up by hundreds, dragged them all from their ship and threw them into chains. The language of these people was unknown to the Northmen, and yet seemed to resemble most the Irish tongue. They understood that thereupon the people of the country deliberated, some condemning the Northmen to death, others to slavery, until an old man of lofty stature and with venerable white hair and a great retinue, before whom a standard was borne, rode up and like a prince was received with the utmost respect. To him thereupon were submitted the opinions of those who had been debating. Having summoned the sailors he addressed them in Danish and asked, whence they came. Having learned that most of them were Icelanders, he asked Gudleif, from what part of Iceland they came. When the latter had mentioned Borgarfjord, he enquired concerning the state and condition of the several nobles there and extending his conversation enquired for Snorre the priest, his sister Thurid and her son Kjartan. When the crowd thereupon interrupted him, demanding that some decision should be come to regarding the ship, he selected twelve men as his council and retired. After considerable delay he addressed Gudleif in the following words: "I have pleaded your cause before my fellow citizens, who consider it a favor that they have left your fate to my decision, and accordingly I grant you permission to depart. Indeed, though summer is far advanced, I advise and urge you to sail hence as soon as possible, for this people is unmanagable and faithless, and will soon be angered on account of the violation of its laws." Then said Gudleif: "What shall I report in my native country? Whom shall I declare my deliverer to be?" "To know that is unnecessary," he answered, "for I do not wish my friends and relatives to be drawn hither through affection for me, lest perchance the same fortune awaits them which you would have met with, had I not intervened; moreover, I am already of such an age that death may overtake me at any moment; but even if it be put off ever so long, there are far away in this land other men more powerful than I, who will certainly not send off strangers unharmed." Thereupon he remained with them, until a favorable breeze sprang up, and to Gudleif, as he departed, he gave a golden ring and a sword, the former to be delivered to Thurid, sister of Snorre the priest, the latter to her son Kjartan, who after his father's death held the manor of Froda. In reply to the question, by whom he should say the gifts were sent, he replied: "by one to whom the sister of the priest Helgafell was dearer than the priest himself had been." But if any one should think that from these words he knows who I am, do you repeat my words that I forbid any one to journey hither; for this land for the most part is harborless, and the people hostile to strangers, no matter where they land, unless perchance as in your case, accident has brought them. Gudleif having taken his ship out of the harbor the same autumn, reached Dublin, whence he had started and there he spent the winter. It is plain that the man was Bjorn, called the champion of Breidavik, who, recorded history relates, served under Palnatoke, then under Stjrbjorn, chief of Suecia (Sweden,) and after his murder a second time under Palnatoke, though in accordance with the established custom of Icelandish writers, the chronology is not treated with care. As a young man, he had fallen in love with Thurid, and was for that reason pursued by her brother, in order to put him to death; after courageously escaping him by his wiles, he permitted himself to be prevailed upon by entreaties, to leave his country;

but to what place the ship which bore him was borne, no one had determined with certainty, before it became known that he had been driven to the place where Gudleif found him; but how this happened has never since been found out. That this country was some part of America, is made likely by the winds which Gudleif met with, by the direction of his voyage and by his departure from and return to Ireland. But as I have made mention in Chapter 8 of the prodigies of Froda and of the woman from the Hebrides by whom, according to the book which Bjorn of Skardza followed, Leif the Lucky is falsely reported to have had a son, and as we have now come to the same manor where these incidents are said to have occurred and the same persons among whom they happened, it is proper to copy the story of them from the history of the Eyrbyggians, and add them here as a finishing touch to our history.

CHAPTER XVII.

OF THE PRODIGIES OF FRODA.

In the first year of the reign of the Jarls Eric and Sven, sons of Hakon, Jarl of the Hladae, prodigies were remarked on a manor in the western quarter of Iceland, called Froda; their cause and origin I shall relate in order. The manor was occupied by a wealthy man called Thorodd, surnamed SKATTKAUPANDI, or the tribute-buyer. For he sold his boat to some shipwrecked men of Orkney who were in danger of life on the coast of Ireland, while bringing tribute money from the Hebrides and Mona (Man) to Earl Sigurd about the year 980, and took for pay a part of the tribute, as has been recounted by us in our History of the Orkneys, chapter 10. His wife was Thurid, the sister of the famous Snorre, priest of Helgafell, whose authority was very great in that part of the island. Thorodd had received in his house a woman, Thorgunna by name, who had come the same summer from Dublin on the invitation of his wife. She was led by the hope of getting possession of the many and valuable treasures which the stranger possessed. This woman was a native of the Hebrides, and was at this time more than fifty years old. However, she would not pay a large sum for Thurid's hospitality, nor sell what was dearer to her than gold, even at the greatest price, though she was worried ever so much by her hostess; she said, she would earn her living by work, but not by low and servile work. On these conditions she was received as a guest. The bed assigned to her she covered with spreads and blankets so precious that nothing more valuable was ever seen in that place. Thurid all the more inflamed with the desire to possess them, offered Thorgunna an immense price, but in vain. She would not sleep on the ground, she answered, even for the sake of Thurid, however respectable a lady she might be. Whenever the weather was unfavorable to drying hay, she worked at embroidery, at other times using her own mattock, she worked at the hay. Her form was tall and she was proportionally stout; her complexion was slightly dark, her eyes large, her hair also was dark and long, and her manners graceful. There was in the same house a certain Thorer Vidlegg, (Wooden-leg) with his wife Thorgrima, called GALDRAKINN, or of the magic chin; he was to be supported at the host's expense by right of relationship, at that time, I believe, still in vogue. Thorgunna and Thorgrima forever quarrelled. Young Kjartan was passionately loved by the stranger Thorgunna, but her passion was unreturned, and she was vexed that she did not please him equally. A rainy summer was followed by a dry autumn. The sky was clear, undotted by even a single cloud, when all bent upon gathering hay, performed each the duty assigned to him by the master. Thorgunna on that day was to dry and gather into sheaves as much hay as would suffice to feed an ox throughout the winter. At one o'clock in the afternoon a cloud arising in the north moved over Thorodd's house and the manor of Froda. From it fell so much rain that it saturated all the hay which had not been put into sheaves, and the sky became so dark that the workmen could not see one another. But when the cloud passed away it was seen that it had rained blood. Then the weather grew clear, and all the blood which had fallen on the hay, dried, except that on Thorgunna's sheaves; nor could the blood which stained the mattock she held, and her garments, be cleansed off. When Thorodd enquired of her, what this prodigy meant, she said she did not know, but that it foreboded the death of somebody who was close to him. Having gone home the same evening and put off the garments that were dripping with blood, she went to bed, repeating that she saw she was detained by sickness. On that evening she would take no food. Early the following morning Thorodd went to her and asked, what she thought would be the issue of her illness. She answered that she would not suffer from disease thereafter, for the present would be her last sickness; that she considered him the wisest man of the manor, and for that reason warned him after her death to dispose of the property owned and left by her, according to her testament or last will; that if this were disregarded it was much to be feared farther prodigies would follow the one that had been seen. But he promised to recognize her as a prophetess and not to disobey her instructions or last will. "My corpse," she replied, "I order to be taken to Skalholt, where I foresee will be for a long time the foremost place in the island; for I hope that the ministers of the gospel are already assembled there, who will perform my obsequies according to the sacred rite. As a reward for your trouble and the outlay which you will make for this purpose, you will take in advance as much of my property as I shall order and with this you can be satisfied. Your wife will take from the undivided property my purple cloak which I dispose of in this manner, that she may submit with equanimity to whatever I provide regarding the rest. My ring the church of Skalholt shall have in payment for my burial; but the coverings of my bed, and my girdles, and all my possessions I command to be burned, for I do not foresee that they will be of any service to any one; and yet I do not do this, because I envy mankind the possession of my property, but because I do not wish men on my account to suffer and be overwhelmed by the many hardships and afflictions which I foresee will follow, if my directions will be disobeyed." Thorodd repeated his former promises. Then her illness began to grow more violent, and after the lapse of a few days it carried her off. The corpse was placed in a coffin and the next day taken to church. Then Thorodd bade all the equipments of her bed to be carried outside and a fire to be lit, into which they were to be thrown. When his wife saw this, she said that things so valuable should not be destroyed; for, said she, her old wives' talk is not of enough importance to make me willing to suffer the loss of these valuables through fear of her threats. And adding entreaties, she urged her husband with such earnestness to preserve the garments, that she saved all the girdles and coverlets from the fire, the neck-cloths, mattrasses and pillows only being consigned to the flames. And yet Thorodd's wife was not satisfied by this concession, though he was vexed at her excessively violent threats. Afterwards the funeral preparations were made and the corpse-bearers were taken to the bier, and men of distinction were selected for the office; special horses too were chosen, for a long journey of many miles was to be gone through. The corpse was wrapped in linen shrouds which were seamless. Straightway they passed through solitudes, nor was anything remarked that was worthy of mention, before they had passed the manor of Valbjarnarvall. There the mire, softened by the rain, hindered their progress. They had crossed with difficulty the river called Nordra in the Eyafjord, for it was filled by the streams which it receives, and which formed pools owing to the long rain storms, and could be crossed only with difficulty, if at all. One evening they came, tired by their long toil, to the manor called Nes, situated in the district of Stafholztung. There, as they were denied a lodging and yet could not proceed further on account of the approaching darkness, they set down their burden and carried the corpse into a house that lay apart. Having entered the dining hall, they intended to pass the night fasting. Though the servants had gone to sleep, they heard a sound as if of a man walking in the store room. Suspecting that there were thieves they ran in, and on opening the door, beheld there a woman tall of stature and naked, and covered by no garment whatsoever, who dealt out food; frightened thereby they dared not approach, and going to the corpse-bearers they related what they had seen. When these had hastened thither they recognized Thorgunna, whose corpse they were carrying, and did not think it safe to meddle with her affairs. When she had got as much food as she thought right, she brought it into the dining-room and placed it on the table. Then the corpse-bearers said to the host: "Perhaps you will regret refusing us food and hospitable kindness." Then the host and his wife replied, that they should have food and whatever they might need. After this assurance Thorgunna departed from the dining room and appeared there no more; but the guests entering took off their wet garments and changed them for dry ones; having signed with the cross the food which Thorgunna had placed there, they partook of it without delay and without any harm to themselves. Having spent the night there, they resumed their journey on the following day, and, wherever they came, they spread the report of this occurrence and obtained what they asked for, as no one dared to refuse them what they needed. At last they arrived at Skalholt and the ring and the other treasures willed by Thorgunna, were delivered to the priests and eagerly accepted by them, and the corpse was committed to earth already consecrated, and the corpse-bearers arrived safe at their homes without any damage.

On the manor of Froda there was an immense kitchen; thence there was an entrance, always open, to the bedchamber, the beds being shut in with hangings on both sides. For after the manner of those times, those buildings were adjoining. Now next to the kitchen were two small buildings, one on each side; in the one dried fish were kept, in the other vessels filled with grain; every evening the hearth was lit to cook food, and near it the household were wont to sit together, before going to sup. Now on the evening when the corpse-bearers returned, whilst the household sat near the hearth, a large moon appeared on the kitchen wall, which moved leftwards through the kitchen. Nor did it recede while they were in the kitchen; it was seen by all alike. Thorodd, the host, asked Thorer Vidlegg what the prodigy meant. He answered that it was called VIDARMANA (which is translated "tree moon") and that it foreboded deaths. This marvel lasted a whole week. Then the shepherd, who had returned home unusually silent and more stern than was his wont, was thought to have come upon some prodigy, for he walked by himself and spoke to himself. This lasted till the first two weeks of winter had passed; then at last, having returned, the shepherd took to his bed, and the following morning he was found dead. After being buried near the church he troubled the living; for Thorer Vidlegg rising from bed one night, went outside; when about to return he noticed that the shepherd near the doors was about to prevent his re-entrance. Striving thereupon to escape he was pursued and seized by the shepherd and thrown down at the door with a great crash. Then taking to bed he lay ill for a long time until he died and was buried near the church. Afterwards he was seen in company with the shepherd to walk the night. Next one of Thorodd's servants after lying ill for three days died. Now the fast that precedes Christmas and begins with the first Sunday of Advent was approaching, although at that time Christmas was not celebrated in Iceland, and already six had died in the same house. One evening the heap of dried fish was heard to be upset, but when it was inspected, it was found in its usual condition. After the Yule feast Thorodd accompanied by five servants, sailed in a large ship to bring home fish; but on the same evening in the kitchen of Froda, a seal's head was seen to start up from the floor. When one of the servant-women saw this, she struck it on the head with a piece of wood, but with every blow it rose higher and turned its eyes towards Thorgunna's bed, which was covered with blankets. One of the hired men assailed the seal with repeated blows, but the seal emerged more and more, until it had stretched out its arms; at the same moment the hired man taken with a fit fell down, and great fear seized the rest. At last young Kjartan smote the seal with a powerful blow. Then it shook its head and turned its eyes hither and thither; thereupon he rained down blows without ceasing, and at each blow the seal sank down and appeared to be about to die, until it was wholly suffocated, and Kjartan struck the earth over its head. All these monsters seemed to fear Kjartan most of all. The following day Thorodd and his companions perished in the waves near the place called Enne, and the ship with the fish was dashed against the shore, but the corpses were not found. When this news was brought home, Kjartan and his mother invited their friends to a funeral feast: the provisions, now used for the funeral banquet, had been intended for the Yule feast. On the first evening of the banquet, when all the guests had taken their seats, Thorodd with his companions, all dripping, entered. This was regarded as a good sign, for the guests were thought to be hospitably received, whenever those who had been drowned came in to the funeral feast celebrated in their honor; for at that time there remained much of the pagan superstition, though the Icelanders were Christians and had been baptized. Thorodd with his men, having passed through the dining hall, made for the kitchen, without answering any one's greeting; finally they all seated themselves near the hearth, the servants fleeing. There these dead men tarried until the fire was covered with ashes; then they departed. On every evening, while the funeral feast lasted, this took place. The guests thought it would cease when the feast had ended. But it turned out very differently. After the guests left, when the servants came to light the hearth, Thorodd with his companions took their seats near it, for they were all dripping wet and with their hands wrang the water out of their clothes. As they sat there, Thorer Vidlegg came from the opposite side with his companions, equal in number to the others and all covered with dust, sat down and he shook the dust from his garments on Thorodd and his companions. But the servants were all driven from their seats on that evening and had no light. The following evening fire was lit in another house, for they hoped that the ghosts would not come there; but the ghosts behaved as before. On the third evening, at Kjartan's suggestion, an oblong hearth was built in the kitchen and a fire lit: but the food was cooked in the small house. This proved successful, for then the servants were not troubled. But Thorodd with his men occupied the kitchen. They heard that the fish in the fish heap were scaled off during the nights. On climbing up the fish heap they saw standing forth a scorched and black tail, like a calf's tail. One man leaping up seized it, and tried to draw it to himself, and called on the rest to do likewise. All the servants of the house, both male and female, ran to draw it out, but it did not permit itself to be stirred and seemed dead. When they used their utmost strength, however, it suddenly slipped from their hands and took the skin from their palms. Thereafter no trace of it was seen; but when they destroyed the heap of fish, they found the fish scaled off. When this was done, Thorgrima Galdrakinn, or of the magic chin, being seized by a sudden sickness, died, and she was seen seated in her husband's company. And now the disease was renewed a second time, after the tail appeared and more women died than men. Six of them were carried off at once by the disease and the ghosts of the dead drove the others away from the house. Of thirty domestics who were alive in the preceding autumn, seven survived in the month of Goa, (a part of which corresponds with February, a part with March.) In this condition of affairs, Kjartan visited his maternal uncle Snorre the priest, and asked his advice. He deputed a priest sent to him by Gissur the White along with his son Thord Kause, accompanied by six others to go with Kjartan and advised them to burn the girdles and all the bed-clothes of Thorgunna and to summon to judgment all the dead that were hostile to the living, and requested the priest to perform his sacred offices, to bless water, and to absolve the servants from their sins. On the eve of the feast of the Purification of the Blessed Virgin, they arrived at Froda, and the neighbors were gathered in the road and summoned to accompany them; on their arrival a fire was lit on the hearth to cook food. Thurid, the mistress of the manor, had at the time been attacked by the same disease of which the rest had perished. Kjartan having entered the kitchen took the coal from the hearth: there he saw his father Thorodd sitting as usual with his companions near the hearth; going out Kjartan destroyed Thorgunna's bed and all her furniture, and burned all her clothes and adornments; then he summoned Thorer Vidlegg to judgment, while Thord Kause called Thorodd, because they had invaded another's house without permission, and deprived the inhabitants of life and strength. Thereupon all that sat at the hearth side were summoned; then judges were appointed at the door and a law-suit instituted as in a law-court, witnesses and proofs were brought forward and repeated at the trial and a final decision given. This having been done, Thorer Vidlegg rising said: "I remained here as long as I was permitted," and he departed by the door where the trial had not been held. Then judgment was pronounced in the shepherd's case, and as soon as he had heard it, he rose and said: "I shall depart now, and I think I should have done so before." And Thorgrima Galdrakinn having heard her sentence answered: "We sat as long as we could," and having said this she left. One by one they were expelled in this way; after saying something, they went forth, unwillingly however, as their words showed. Thorodd, the lord of the manor was condemned last, and hearing the decision rose and said: "Few of us are left, let us all flee." And so he was the last to leave the house.

Then Kjartan with the rest entered the house; but the priest sprinkled the several parts of the house with holy water, and on the following day celebrated mass and the sacred rites, and thereafter the dead no longer infested it, and Thurid, the mistress of the house, recovered.

Here we may remark the devil's cunning and his power over those, who either do not know the true religion or are less instructed in the articles of faith; for nowhere do we read that anything similar happened on that island, after the true light of the Gospel rose and enlightened its inhabitants.

ADDENDA.

I translated that the sun at the time of the solstice, rose in Vinland about nine o'clock and set at three; I shall give my reasons for doing so. But as other reasons occurred to me afterwards, that stirred up doubt on this question, I shall leave both to be weighed by the unprejudiced reader. For after this History of Vinland was returned to me in print, I began to examine these points again and again, because the position of the land seemed to be nowise compatible with the fertility there described, and this was especially the case after the Swedish translation of the History of the Norse Kings called HEIMS KRINGLA, published by the distinguished John Peringskiold came into my hands. For following the interpretation of the learned Gudmund Olafson, he translated this passage differently; for both, adhering strictly to the rules of the grammarinns and translating word for word, understood it otherwise than I did, and yet did not catch the author's meaning any better. For the author, though he does not refer the latitude of the land to any precise degree of the equinoctial line, nevertheless left this to be clearly inferred from the rising and setting of the sun in winter and would have left it more clearly stated, if he had found it more carefully described. He certainly used clear language, as it appeared to me. The passage reads as follows in the 105th chapter of the Swedish edition, page 331 : *Meira var par jafndaegri enn a Graenlandi eda Islandi, sol hafdi par eykturstad, og damalastad um Skammdeigi.*" The meaning of these words the distinguished Arngrim Jonas, in the ninth chapter of his Greenland expounds as follows: In that place there is no such winter, or cold, nor is the winter solstice the same as in Iceland or Greenland, the sun remaining above the horizon about six hours (for they had no sun-dials.) This meaning I found myself long before seeing the work of Arngrim Jonas, firstly from the information of Brynjolf

Svenonson (if I understood him correctly), the most learned of the bishops of Skalholt up to his own time, a man without peer, to whom as a youth I was sent in the year 1662 with royal letters by my most clement Lord, the best of Kings, Frederick III, to learn the true signification of the most difficult ancient words and phrases, and secondly from the relation of sunrise to sunset as will be shown presently. Now I shall examine Peringskjold's interpretation. "The day too," says he "is longer than in Greenland and in Iceland for the sun there had periods of increase, and day-light appeared about breakfast time (six or seven o'clock) when the day was shortest." From this explanation we learn nothing certain of the position of the country. Peringskjold was led astray by the word EYKT, which usually means a space of three hours, but in another sense expresses the third hour after noon, which is also called NON. Explaining the author in the first sense, he showed nothing peculiar: for no longer periods of increase belong to the sun there than elsewhere. Nor have we here a single word about day-light, that is to say, dawn, but there is question of sunrise and sunset; nor, in my opinion, did the Icelanders breakfast at six or seven o'clock, but at nine o'clock, which they call DAGMAL. I should translate the author's words as follows: "There (in Vinland) the winter days are always longer than in Greenland or Iceland, the sun there touched the third hour afternoon and the ninth before noon." Here the words sunset and sunrise are so explained, that even if the word EYKT were unknown in the latter sense, yet its meaning could easily be deduced from its connection with the ninth hour before noon and the meaning of the word Dagmal, which always denotes that hour, as well as from the relation of sunrise to sunset and its connection with the third hour.

This view is confirmed from the ancient division of the natural day customary among the Icelanders: for the day is divided into eight parts according to the time the sun passes in each. For they call NATTMAL the part of the day while the sun is in the northwest, LAGNAETTE, while it is in the north, OTTA or RISMAL, *i. e.*, dawn or rising time, whilst it is in the northeast, MIDUR MORGUN, while it is in the east, DAGMAL, while it is in the southeast, HADEIGI, while it is in the south, NON, while it is in the southwest, MIDURAFTAN, while it is in the west.

Convinced by these arguments, I placed Vinland in Estotiland; but when I judged again and again that the products of the country (Vinland) did not suit the climate of Estotiland I began to examine the Swedish version more carefully, and especially to enquire more diligently into the meaning of the word EYKT, suspecting that this word led astray the Swedish translator. Finding it in no dictionaries, except that of Gudmund Andreson, and there set down only with the former meaning, I began to study the most ancient Canon Law of the Icelanders. From its ninth chapter I copy the following words: "*Ver skulum hallda Laugardag enn siounda hvern nonhelgan, sa er naest Drottinsdeigi firir, paskal ei vinna upp fra eykt, nema pat er nu man ec telia, pat a at, vinna allt er drottinsdag a at vinna. Pa er eykt er ut sudrs aept er deilld i pridiunga, og hefir Solinn geingna tvo luti, enn einn ogeingin.*" These words we translate as follows: "We shall hold sacred every seventh day, that is to say, the Sabbath, (Saturday) up to the Nona. This immediately precedes Sunday. Then from the EYKT hour it is not allowed to work, except for those things which I shall now mention: then all those things must be prepared which are necessary for Sunday. By EYKT is meant the time when the heavens between south and west are divided into three parts and the sun has completed two parts, whilst the third remains." I had written that the description of Vinland had explained this in clear words, but now I find that it has entangled that narrative, which the present passage made even more difficult. For the word NON denoted three o'clock after noon both in Iceland and formerly among the Anglo-Saxons; and from the establishment of the Christian religion or from the passage of this very law every generation in Norway so understood this word, and to-day in accordance with this rule the Norse rest on Saturdays. The present passage likewise illustrates it, inasmuch as it bids the sanctification to begin from NON and work to cease at EYKT; thence some may wish to infer that NON and EYKT are synonyms and that they designate the hour so often mentioned. But how far the very description of the same differs from this opinion, everybody sees. For the space through which the sun passes from midday to sundown, requires six hours, a third of which makes two hours. Two-thirds end at four o'clock after noon. If EYKT and NON are to be understood to mean this hour, in the first place the most ancient and most generally accepted division of hours falls to the ground, each of which, like the canonical hours, includes three common hours. The connection with the hour, DAGMAL, also disappears, for this designates nine o'clock before noon. Now it is not possible that on the day of the winter-solstice the sun should set at four o'clock in the afternoon and rise at nine o'clock in the forenoon; for it really rises at eight o'clock, and the day from sunrise to sundown is lengthened to eight hours. If then the words EYKT and NON mean the same thing, and signify the fourth hour, Dagmal is not nine o'clock, but must be advanced to eight o'clock, and consequently Vinland lies under the forty-ninth degree, and its shortest day measures eight hours; and this position certainly fits its products better than the position of Estotiland. We read that among the Romans NONA had not always the same meaning; for, as appears from the ancient manuscript of the Manerii, it sometimes meant midday. But the NONA of the clocks in most ancient times meant the last hour, when the sun was already setting (see Hofm. lex. at the word NONA); in like manner it might mean among us also, hours different from three o'clock after noon. As to the word DAGMAL, Gudmund Andreson in his lexicon supports our present view; for by Dagmal he understands, not nine o'clock before noon according to the received use of the word, but eight o'clock, which corresponds precisely with the sun's setting at four o'clock after noon; aud I doubt not that he wrote this supported by some authority; but whence he got, it I am not yet clear. However that may be, the explanation of our manuscript which translates the word EYKT by four o'clock, claims for itself undoubted authority, whether EYKT means the same thing as NON or not. As I said before, I leave these points to be examined by the judgment of the intelligent reader, and first of all he must decide, whether public prayers were said from three o'clock, that is to say, NON, to four o'clock, and then, whether the holiday began at four o'clock, *i. e.*, EYKT; this being settled, everything is consistent, and we recognize in the land, which to-day under the name TERRE NEUVE or TERRA NOVA on the adjacent continent on the coast of Canada has been reduced under the power of the French, the ancient Vinland. But if the position of the places which is here set forth, be compared more carefully with the character of those countries, I doubt not but that everything will be more clearly understood by those who either inhabit them or visit them purposely.

On page 61, after line 23, insert: After writing the foregoing I received Heimskringla, or History of the Norse Kings, translated by Joh. Peringskjold, printed at Stockholm, 1697, and find from chapter 103 to chapter 115 matter which is found in neither of the authentic copies of the Church of the Most Holy Trinity, the KRINGLA or the JOFRASKINNA. They are taken either from copies of the History of Olaf Triggeson or from some other source.

INDEX.

Adam of Bremen 60
Albania, or Great Ireland .. 7, 14, 61
Alftafjord 49
Ananias, J. L 12
Andefort 13
Are Marson 61
Arnestap 44
Arnora 43
Astrutharson, Sven 60
Audr, Queen 43
Aurlig 62
Avalldainna 58

Barthol, Thomas 45
Berius, Ivar 17
Bjarne 25, 26, 53
Bjarne, Bishop 40
Bjarn of Breidavik 15, 64
Bjarne, the Icelander 9, 25
Bjarne Grimolfson 49
Bjarney Islands 51
Bjorn of Skardsa ... 7, 9, 10, 34, 37
 40, 62, 65
Bjorn Buna 62
Bleyker 12
Bondendon 13
Borgarfjord 63
Boterus, John 13
Brand, Bishop 40
Brattahlide 29, 47, 50
Breidafjord 49
Bremen, Adam of 14
Buno 10, 11, 13

Cabaru 13
Campo 13
Canada 10
Cape Hull 30
Cartier, Jacques 13
Cluverius, Philip 10, 15
Codex Flateyensis .. 7, 9, 10, 29, 31,
 32, 40, 47, 49, 50
Columbus, Christopher 15, 16
Crodme 13

Dagmal 76, 78
Davis' Straits 4
Dithmar, Bishop of Merseburg ... 64

Doffais 13
Drogio 11
Dublin 63, 64
Duime 13

Einar of Langabrekka 43
Enior 59
Eric II 16
Eric, first Bishop of Greenland .15,62
Eric the Red ... 9, 25, 30, 32, 41, 42,
 43, 47, 49, 50, 61, 65
Eric and Sven 30, 65
Eriksfjord 29, 33, 34, 39, 43, 47,
 49, 65
Erlend the Strong 59
Espishol 59
Estland 14
Estotiland 10, 11, 77, 78
Eykt 76, 77, 78
Eyrbyggva Saga 41

Flose 59
Frederick III 12, 76
Frederick IV 3
Freidis 10, 37, 38, 51, 53
Frisland 11, 12, 13
Froda 41, 65, 69, 72
Furdustrand 52

Gamlason, Thorhall 49
Gardar 37
Gissur the White 72
Glaumba 40
Gnup 92
Greenland ... 4, 17, 25, 26, 39, 41, 43,
 44, 46, 49, 50, 51, 65
Grimhilde 33, 47
Grimkel 62
Grimolfson, Bjarne 49, 58
Grisland 14
Grund 59
Gudleif Gunnlaugson 63, 64
Gudleif 65
Gudmund Olafson 75
Gudmund Andreson 78
Gudrid 29, 32, 33, 34, 43, 46, 47,
 48, 49, 50, 65
Gudrun, wife of Jorund 59

INDEX

Gunnlaug 59
Gunnlaugson, Gudleif 63, 64

Hacon, Eric 26
Hake..... 52
Hekja..... 52
Hako........ 6
Hakon, Earl 65
Halla 59
Hallbera.. 59
Halldise....................... 44
Hallfrid 40
Hellveiga 43
Harold the Bold, or Haughty.... 16, 40, 60
Hauk 7, 40, 41, 59
Heimskringla................75, 79
Hebrides. . ... .65
Helluland................27, 51
Henry VII................16
Herjulf............25
Herjulfsnes............25, 26, 44, 47
Hjorleif......................62
Hondius..................13
Hrafn...................... 61
Hrap......................62
Hudson Bay......... 11
Hvitra Manna Land... ......14, 58

Ibini................. 13
Icaria................... 14
Iceland 39, 44, 65
Ilofo.. 13
Ingibjorg................59
Ingveld....................40
Ireland.............53, 58, 65

Jedeve, ...13
Jonas, Arngrim......... 13, 40, 75
Jonas, the Breton..............13
Jones, Jonas or John an Irish Bishop 14
Jones or Johannes, Bishop 62
Jorund.....................62

Karlsefne.... 10, 35, 36, 37, 39, 50, 51, 53, 54, 57, 59
Kelldum...............59
Ketill................59
Ketil, Flatnesi.................. 62
Kios....................62
Kipping, Henry............11, 13
Kjalarnes. 30, 52, 53, 54, 62
Kjartan 66, 71, 72, 73
Kornhjalm af tre..............30
Kringla or Jofraskinna.... .. 7, 79

Krossanes 32

Lagnaette..................... 76
Landnama Book............ 62
Leif.... .. 9, 30, 32, 37, 41, 42, 51
Leif of Brattahlide.... 26, 27, 29, 34
Lery, Baron de........ 15
Limerick................61
Lisufjord..................47
Lysufjord 32

Madoc 6
Magin, John A.......... 13
Mar.... 62
Markland............27, 51, 57
Marson, Are 14, 61
Martinerius..................12
Mausur................. 29
Mercator..................13
Mikiunes........ 54
Miritius, John..........13
Monaco........ 13

Nattmal. 76
Nes................. 68
Nordra..................68
Norumbega 15

Ocibar..... 13
Olafson, Gudmund............75
Olaf Triggvin, Trygveson 7, 42, 52, 53
Orm.....................44
Ortelius 13
Otta or Rismal 76

Palnatoke 64
Peringskjold, John........7, 76, 79
Porlanda..... 13

Rane...................13
Reid, Whale 34
Reikyanes........ .. ..14, 61
Reinarnes..................59
Reinenes Monastery........ . 59
Reykjadal................62
Rolf.................16
Rome....................33, 40
Rovea..................13
Rudbecke, Olaf.......... 8, 12, 60
Runoff......................40

Samoyeds..................17
Sanestol....................13
Sanson d' Abbeville.. . ... ,11, 15
Schalholt..................14
Sigmund...................43

INDEX.

Sigrid............................47, 48
Sigurd Earl........................65
Skagafjord.........................40
Skalholt...........................69
Skialg Ulf.........................14
Skogastrand........................49
Skraelings......10, 11, 17, 31, 35, 36
                              53, 54, 57
Snorre..............40, 51, 53, 57, 59
Snorre, priest of Helgafell...63, 64,
                                  65, 72
Snorre Thorbrandson................49
Sorand.............................13
Spakonfellzhofde...................34
Spirige............................13
Stafholztung.......................68
Steinvor...........................59
Stjrbjorn..........................64
St. Olaf...........................63
Straumsfjord.......................54
Straumsey..........................54
Streme.............................13
Sturleson, Snorro...................7
Sven Astritharson..................60
Svenonson, Brynjolf................75

Terre Neuve........................79
Thistel............................43
Thistilsfjord......................43
Thorer..................29, 32, 47, 59
Thorer of Steige...................40
Thorer Vidlegg.........66, 70, 71, 73
Thorana............................40
Thorbjorg..........................44
Thorbjorg Knarrabringa.............62
Thorbjorn..................29, 43, 47
Thorbjorn of Stockanes.........49, 65
Thorbjorn Vifillson............43, 47
Thorbrandson, Snorre...............49
Thord of Hesthofde.................34
Thord Kause........................73
Thordis............................59
Thorfinn, Earl of the Orkneys...14,
                                  16, 61
Thorfinn, Karlsefne....34, 49, 59, 65
Thorgeir.......................40, 43
Thorgerde..........................25

Thorgils...........................41
Thorgaima Galdradinn...........72, 73
Thorgunna......66, 67, 69, 70, 72, 73
Thorhall....................51, 53, 54
Thorhall Gamlason..................49
Thorhild or Thiodhild..........61, 62
Thorhilde..................41, 42, 43
Thorhilde Riupa....................34
Thorkel............................44
Thorkell Geiterson.................61
Thorlak, Bishop....................40
Thorlake, Theodore.................13
Thorodd........65, 67, 68, 70, 71, 73
Thorstein Ericson....10, 32, 33, 41,
                          42, 47, 48, 65, 69
Thorstein the Black................33
Thorstein the Red..................43
Thorstein Ranglat..................59
Thorstein, Surt....................32
Thorvald Krok......................59
Thorvald............9, 10, 29, 30, 31, 32
Thorvald Ericson...................57
Thorvard...........................51
Thurid.................63, 64, 65, 66, 73
Tyrker.........................27, 28

Ulf Skialg.........................62

Vabjarnavall.......................68
Vaege..............................58
Valgerdis..........................59
Valdidida..........................58
Valthiof...........................62
Venai..............................13
Vesputius, Americus.................6
Vestri, Bygd.......................17
Vetthilde..........................58
Vifill.............................43
Vifillson, Thorbjorn...........43, 47
Vifilsdal..........................43
Vinland........4, 7, 14, 16, 25, 29, 30,
                      34, 37, 39, 51, 61, 63, 77
White Man's Land...............57, 61
Winland............................60

Zeni, the.......................6, 11
Zichinnus..........................12

www.ingramcontent.com/pod-product-compliance
Lightning Source LLC
Chambersburg PA
CBHW031121160426
43192CB00008B/1072